A Man Called Rasmus

By

JAMES T. BORN

authorHOUSE®

AuthorHouse™
1663 Liberty Drive
Bloomington, IN 47403
www.authorhouse.com
Phone: 1-800-839-8640

Published by AuthorHouse   07/09/2012

ISBN: 978-1-4772-1164-9 (sc)
ISBN: 978-1-4772-1165-6 (e)

Library of Congress Control Number: 2012909489

ABOUT THIS BOOK

An historical account of a man who left his home in Norway, and came to America, in search of a new way of life. It is about his journeys and adventures, as he took up arms, and bravely fought in the 1862 Indian Wars, and in the U.S. Civil War. You will not want to put this book down, once you start reading it.   *Author*

A MAN CALLED RASMUS

A MOMENT IN TIME

BIOGRAPHY OF RASMUS OLSON   1825-1893
By His Great-Great Grandson
JAMES T. BORN

Contents

THE LEGACY OF AN AMERICAN HERO

Born Family Genealogical History

Volume One

"A man lives as long . . . . as he is remembered"

Your tombstone stands among the rest; neglected and
alone.
The name and date are chiseled out
on polished, marbled stone. It reaches out to all who care
It is too late to mourn. You did not know that I exist
You died and I was born.
Yet each of us are cells of you
In flesh, in blood, in bone.
Our blood contracts and
Beats a pulse
Entirely not our own.
Dear Ancestor, the place
You filled
Over one hundred years ago
spreads out among the ones you left
Who would have loved you so.
I wonder if you lived and
Loved,
I wonder if you knew
that someday I would find
This spot, and come to visit you.

Author unknown

IN PURSUIT OF WHO I AM

In the year 2002, I came upon a reasoning to try and find out the nature of my genes. To discovery that great mystery that we all, at one time or another, ask ourselves, "Who am I "?

I often wondered of whom I took after more, was it my father or my mother? I ask myself, why do I have blue eyes, why did I have dark brown hair, why at 65 years of age, do I only have slight wisps of gray hair showing, while at the same time my friends have no hair, or all gray hair, why do doctor's tell me that I have thick skin, why am I with large shoulders and have unusual strength and a host of other thoughts about my being that seem to defy my knowledge and general understanding?

*My quest for these answers came through a mature understanding of the mixing of blood, at the time of conception, and by researching scientific developments over the last twenty years or so, what I have come to realize is that our genes or genetic makeup, is passed down through inheritance, in the form of **D**eoxyribose **N**ucleic **A**cid "DNA", from parents to sibling, and as it does, it encodes all generic information from both parents, while it continues to maintain prior passed down genetic information from our ancestors. This in essence makes up who we are.*

When we realize this, we also must realize that we have within us DNA traits, handed down, not just from or parents, but from their parents, grandparents and their ancestors before them. Our blood has become a historical library, and guiding force of our life. Blood really is thicker than water.

In perspective, it is a scientific rule that matter can not be destroyed nor created. We are all made of matter. Knowing this prompts me to believe that matter from our ancestors is alive in you and is alive in me.

I wanted to know what country they came from, when were they born, and what did they die from? What experiences did they have, what obstacles in life did they pass through?

What was happening in the world during their life time? How did they live and what did they look like, did they look like me? Do I have similar medical conditions or passed down medical conditions, that I should watch out for in me, or in my offspring?

Did my relatives have children that may have generated to where I have cousins or other unknown kin? What were their interests and occupations? Were any of them famous of infamous?

Did they fight for their country and believe in the very same things that I believe in? In what ways are we alike?

These and countless other questions have come to light during my genealogical research. I have and shall endeavor to print as many facts as possible. This work of course is not finished.

This is the reason why I will continue the thrill of discovery and the quest to understand who I am.

Their blood is in me, as your ancestors blood is in you. One must remember that only God can create matter. Matter is what we are all made of. God will not destroy that what he created. If he wanted to destroy his creations, than why did he not destroy Satan and his legions of devils, of whom he cast out of Heaven?

Even they will continue to exist, when God finally casts them into the Lake of Fire, where they will burn forever (King James Version of the Holy Bible, the Book of Revelations 20:10-15).

It is my hopes that all of my descendants, even those yet to be born, will forevermore continue to record the heritage of this family. Maybe someday, one will stand before my gravestone and say thank you.

James T. Born

THE SEED IS THE LIFE

'I planted some hollyhock seed by the garden wall—Some grew small and some grew tall, Some grew red and some grew white, But they all grew for your delight".

There are a few people who do not know their fathers name; then there are a great many who do not know the name of their grandfather; and then there is a countless host of people who do not know the name of their great-grandfather; Perhaps there is only one in a million who can name a dozen ancestors in succession. People who do not care for their ancestors often lack the knowledge of the present-day conditions and future prospects. The student who knows the past all most knows the future' for in today already walks to-morrow. Proper pride of our forebears should make us humble and grateful. It should inspire us all to cut a new notch in the totem pole of fame.

Issac Wagner 1928

Preface and Acknowledgments

"A Man Called Rasmus" is based on fact. It is taken from reliable internet sources, from various public documents, from my family history, and historical letters. The photographs in this book are that of the author's, however, whenever possible, photographs and drawings are included that are not the property of the author and credit and thanks were herein noted to their source. A lot of information was found in, genealogical reports, statements of actual survivors of the various battles, documents found in the United States National Archives, National Park Service, Census Bureau and the United States Department of the Army, Military Records Achieves. The State of Minnesota, State of North Dakota and the State of Alabama, historical records, provided much of the smaller details and information. Other research materials were extracted from various historical societies, Harpers Weekly and from various county and city records. The events noted in this book are as accurate as possible, and stand to serve to honor my Great-Great Grandfather Rasmus Olson. God Bless America and God Bless those who gave it all for our freedom.

When I was a young man growing up in California, I used to sit and talk with my grandmother (on my mothers side of the family), Mabel Rena Christensen (Nelson) (January 17, 1885 to May 19, 1979).

Grandma Mabel
Circa 1903
Family Album

She was a wonderful person, in every since of the word, a real grandmother, in every respect. I was impressed with her stamina and wonderful humor that she displayed in everything she did. When she passed away in 1979, I was devastated. She was 94 years old and throughout her lifetime was witness to history that I can only imagine. As example, when she was almost two years old, the Statue of Liberty was constructed in New York City.

She was eighteen years old when the Wright Brothers flew the first airplane (1903) and was 23 years old when Henry Ford invented the Model T car (1908). What was hard for me to comprehend is that she was born at a time when western towns had shootouts in the streets, outlaws were robbing trains and banks, and famous lawmen like Wyatt Earp were taking care of business, western style in the old west.

The most amazing thing is that on July 20, 1969, Grandma witnessed the Apollo 11 spacecraft land on the moon and man's first footsteps on the moons surface. On that moment, her history went from experiencing covered wagon travel to space exploration.

Grandma's mother was Olive Elizabeth Olson, who was the daughter of Rasmus and Caroline Olson. If only I could have sat with them and talked.

In 2002, I began researching my family roots, using genealogy programs like ancestry.com. The deeper I went into it the more I became addicted to wanting to know more about who I am. I wanted to know the joys and tribulations that those before me went through, I wanted to know about my blood line, why my nose and other body parts are shaped the way they are, why I seemed to possess an unnatural strength, why my demeanor is as it is, why I have always stood against evil, and again a thousand other why's?

As I progressed through my family history, I found a lot of answers to those questions, and many more yet expressed. In my search for parallels with my relatives, I began to concentrate on Olive's father, my Great-Great Grandfather, Rasmus Olson.

Rasmus was an immigrant from Norway, he had no roots or responsibilities to the United States, whatsoever. He was a man who lied about his age at enlistment, by saying that he was born in 1827, instead of his real birth year of 1825. Those extra two years qualified him for enlistment into the United States Army.

Rasmus had that special spirit that so many old country immigrants had when they first came to this great country of ours. They more often than not, had a dangerous journey along the way, just to get here. Many of them lost loved ones to the great perils of the sea, while crossing, some to illness and some to Indians, who were just protecting what was theirs in the first place.

If you were able to talk to most any one of those brave immigrants today, they would likely tell you that they came to America with a dream, that they wanted to make a new life for themselves, and for their families. They would tell you that they wanted to make America part of their life, where one can be free of terrorism and where one can scratch out a living from its rich soil, to fill their bellies. Where one can live in harmony, peace and safety. They would also tell you that freedom isn't free and that it takes sacrifices to keep it. If it was not for their unselfish sacrifices, America would not be as strong as she is today. This is the story of one of those unsung hero's, my Great-Great Grandfather.

DEDICATED TO THE LOVING MEMORY OF
MY MOTHER

Helen Marjorie Born (Christensen)
1921-2008

Great Granddaughter of Rasmus Olson
Family Album

RASMUS OLSON

November 22, 1826-November 22, 1893

Circa 1875

Family Album

Chapter One

RASMUS THE MAN

Rasmus was born on a cold winter day, on November 22, 1826, in a small fishing village in the heart of Norway. Located nestled in a wind protected harbor, surrounded on three sides by the Trondheim Fjord, on Norway's west coast. The name of the township is Frosta. Frosta is located in Nord-Trondelag County. Rasmus was originally given the name of Erasmus. I believe that when Rasmus later came through U.S. Customs, upon his arrival to America, that his name was changed by the screener, to be more Americanized, as was common at that time. To avoid any confusion and out of respect for the name he liked to be known by, I will hereafter use the name of Rasmus in my story.

Rasmus's parents were his father, Ole Olson Wigen and his mother, Lisbeth Jonsdater Person, born 1807. As a historical mention, in 2010, during the construction of a new boat marina, where Rasmus was born, logs were found standing straight up at waters edge. Further investigation of these mysterious logs revealed that they dated to the year 1000. The scientific survey concluded that Frosta is home to Norway's oldest Viking harbor. Frosta also has the distinction of having the oldest church in Norway. The church is called Frostatinget, which was built in the year 1207. Little is known about Rasmus during his early years. We know that he was a Lutheran by faith. The town of Frosta held a rich history which passed down to it's proud people. They were all descendants of the Vikings. A once proud people that brought both fear and prosperity to Europe. They were a race of people that for the most part, lived on the coastal regions of their country. Vikings were famous for the building of Long ships. The craftsman-ship that went into producing these vessels was the main reason that they survived the rigors of the North Atlantic Ocean. Norwegians were great ship builders and sailors, such was their culture and fame.

These vessels were made with flat bottom hulls so they could easily maneuver along the coast and up rivers and land on beaches without tipping over. They carried a large number of warriors and often traveled in small fleets. For the protection of the passengers, large hand held, painted shields were placed along both sides of the boats rail. The Viking warriors painted each one with their various clan symbols. These boats were sleek and fast under sail.

There was no better seamen in the whole of the world than that of the Vikings and in my opinion even that of the Venetian Empire. The Vikings had two reputations, one being that they are known mostly for their warrior nature. They were pirates that raided and looted foreign lands and brought the plunder back with them. They were fierce looking, with horned metal helmets, animal skins about their bodies and huge swords in hand. That life style all but stopped when their King, Harold Hardrade unsuccessfully tried to conquer England in the year 1066. There can be little doubt that Rasmus carried the blood, guts and stamina of those warriors.

The Vikings were also known as industrialist and explores. Between the year 879 and 920, through journeys of discovery, the Vikings found and colonized Iceland and Greenland. They are also know for founding Normandy France and Dublin, Ireland. The Vikings brought trade to several countries, and that in turn brought prosperity to everyone. This is the legacy that Rasmus was born into.

RASMUS OLSON circa 1880 Family Album

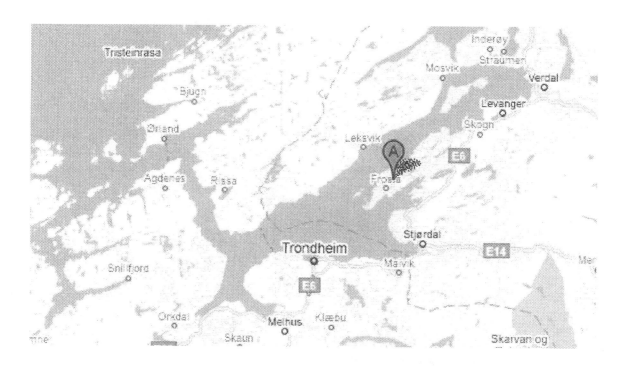

MAP LOCATION FROSTA, NORWAY
Courtesy Google maps

Chapter Two

THE JOURNEY TO AMERICA

On or about March of 1849, Rasmus, then 23 years old, said good bye to his family in Frosta, Norway, and traveled 564 miles south to the sea port of Stravenger, Norway. He paid passage in passenger steerage and boarded the schooner, sailing vessel, Ebenezer, recorded as passenger #30 out of 74.

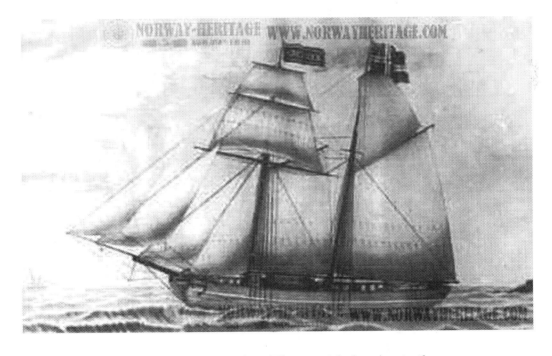

Photograph of drawing (Ebenezer) belonging to the
Stravenger Sjofarts Museum in Norway—Heritage Norway

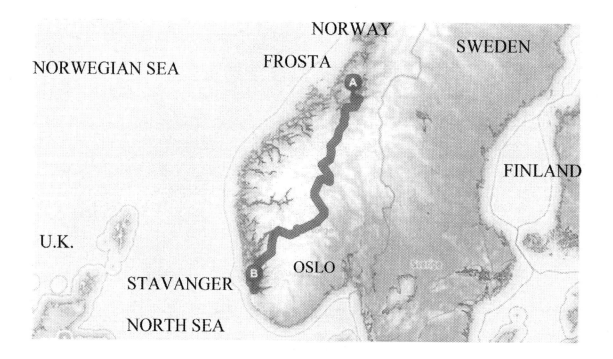

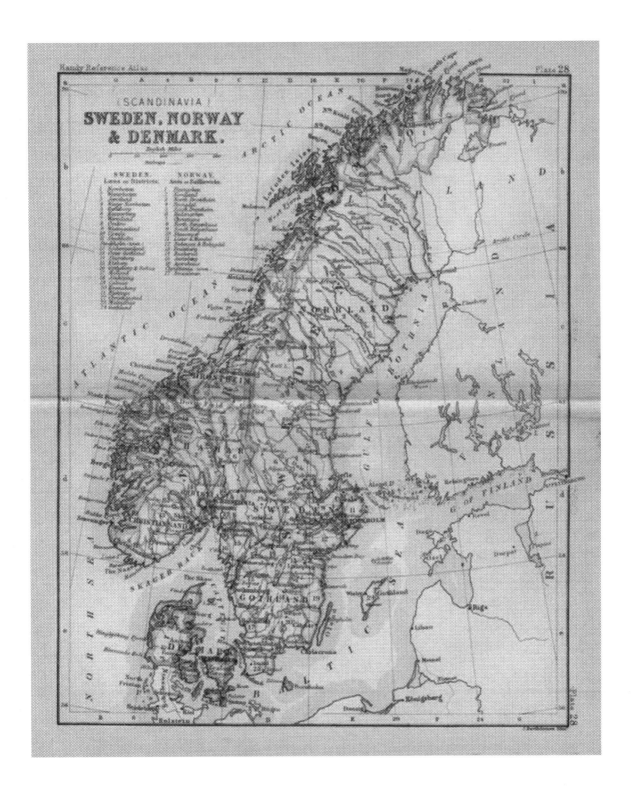

The Ebenezer was a new, 199 ton sailing vessel, built in 1847, by Jacob Kielland and Sons Ship-yard, in Knud Kaisen, Norway. The Captain was H.C. Clausen, an experienced captain who made the passage to America five times. She was considered as one of the smallest and fastest Norwegian emigrant ships in her day.

The transatlantic journey required that every passenger had to bring his own food, which was stored between-decks. Every day the passengers had to fetch his or her own provisions and wait in line to cook them, in one of normally, two cooking pots. Everyone shared these cooking pots. Because fire was a major concern aboard ship, a bin was built on deck and filled with a foot and a half of sand. From here the logs burned to heat the pots. There was no chimney and the smoke often overtook the crew and passengers. Each passenger was required to bring enough food for ten weeks. If he reported to the ships officer with less than that, they would not be allowed to make the journey. Firewood was provided by the ship and was thinly cut.

A TYPICAL 10 WEEK SUPPLY OF FOOD
ONE ADULT

70 Pounds of Hard Bread
8 Pounds of Butter
24 Pounds of Meat
10 Pounds of Side Pork
1 Small Keg of Herring
24 Pounds of Potatoes
20 Pounds of Rye and Barley Flour
1/2 Bushel of Dried Peas
1/2 Bushel of Pearl Barley
3 Pounds of Coffee
3 Pounds of Sugar
2 1/2 Pounds of Syrup
Quantities of salt, Pepper, Vinegar and Onions

Water was provided by the ships Captain. It was stored in kegs below decks, for his rationing. Each passenger was rationed three quarts a day. That amount of water included water for drinking, cooking, and an allocation of small quantities of water for use in personal hygiene.

OTHER ITEMS REQUIRED BY EACH PASSENGER

Blankets
Pillow
Sufficient changes of clothing
Water Pail
Cooking Pot
Coffee Kettle
Dishes
Eating Utensils
Personal Hygiene items like a comb or brush, wash cloths, herbal medicines, and other such items

The burden of having to pack, haul and personally carry on board the ship, their food, the necessity items above and some personal items, like memorabilia and valuables, restricted the allocated storage for each passenger. On a small ship like the Ebenezer, with 74 passengers, there was very little room for personal items to be brought on board. When Rasmus came to America he was one of those poor emigrants, that had to leave so much behind in the old country and arrived in the new world with little more than the cloths on his back.

Above Drawing of Steerage Passengers Embarking
Below CROSS SECTION DRAWING OF SAILING SHIP DECKS
NOTE FOOD STORAGE BETWEEN DECKS
Property of Norway Heritage

The voyage to America, was for the most part, miserable for the passengers. The North Sea was at times violent, with huge waves knocking the ship from side to side, making cooking next to impossible. Fires were not allowed when the seas were rough, so many didn't eat. The first week or so saw most passengers suffering from seasickness. The smell of vomit below the un-vented decks and passenger compartment was overpowering. Crewmen would take a hot iron and dip it in tar, go below decks and let the smoke from the tar permeate the spaces in order to mask the smell. Many people died during these crossings, although no one died on the Ebenezer during Rasmus's crossing.

Because the sea is often unpredictable, at times food and water would run out. This was because the winds, in which the ships depended on for power, were calmer than expected, extending the ships time at sea. At times the food would go bad from salt water intrusion, extending the voyage. Food was often contaminated with salt water, mold or simply went bad.

Rodents (Wharf Rats) were another problem aboard ship. When the ship was in port, they climbed aboard the ship via the mooring lines. They would cause the food to go bad because they would eat through the sacks. That let in moisture and insects. They had the run of the ship and were known to bite humans and leave their waste in the food storage and birthing quarters. When one had to use the toilet, you sat on a special ring seat which hung off the side of the ship, depositing directly into the sea. There was no toilet paper so everyone shared the same sponge, which you had to clean with sea water. Your personal privacy from other passengers or the ships crew, were to say the least, non existent. The emigrants would drop buckets into the sea to draw sea water, to be used to wash there clothing. Sea water often caused body rashes.

There were no doctors or dentists on board the ship to help the crew or its passengers. If you fell and required stitch's, the ships Boatswains Mate would use a sail needle and sail twine to sew you up. Other than rum there was no antiseptic or pain killer of any kind.

If a loved one passed away, the body was sewn into a canvas bag by the Boatswains Mate, and the ships Captain held services, while dumping the body into the sea. Such were the trials and tribulations that our forefathers faced when they came to America.

On April 26,1849, the Ebinezer set sail from Stevenger, Norway. The typical route of travel at that time brought the ship south through the North Sea, down the straights between England and France, (English Channel) through the Celtic Sea and onto the Atlantic Ocean, towards New York. Once the ship left the coast of England, there was no harborage, from there all the way to New York harbor. The ship arrived in New York harbor, without incident, on June 15, 1849.

Passengers arriving in New York were processed through Ellis Island. As the passengers would file past the Custom Officers, the officers often changed the emigrants name. At times, the spelling and their pronunciation. This was done in order for the emigrants to fit into the American culture.

I believe, through my research, that the Immigration Officers at Ellis Island, changed his given name of Erasmus Ollsen to Rasmus Olson. Other accurate information came from U.S. Census postings. Some would display Rasmus as being born in Sweden and others show him born in Norway. For the record, he was born in Norway. Norway and Sweden geographically are side by side and have a history of name changing. Old geographic maps often identified the two as "Sweden". Rasmus was however born in Norway.

After arriving at New York Harbor, Rasmus traveled west to Saint Louis, going through Pennsylvania, Ohio, Indiana and Illinois. The route traveled was well marked by previous wagon trains. It also was a dangerous journey because of the constant threat of Indian attacks, lack of food and of course, disease. Many early pioneers were buried along the trail. When he arrived in Saint Louis, things went from bad to worse as the city was in the middle of a Cholera outbreak, that killed 7,000 people, one tenth of the entire population of Saint Louis.

Rasmus booked passage through the Galena, Dubuque and Minnesota Packet Company, on a steamer boat headed for Saint Paul, Minnesota, via the Mississippi river, an estimated 500 mile trip. This boat was 121 tons, captained by Captain Orren Smith, a long time experienced river pilot. Based upon accounts of boats arriving in Saint Paul, it would appear that the name of his ship was the "Senator". These were flat bottom, steam driven, side-wheel, wooden hull boats. They carried passengers and cargo to various settlements along the river. The river was in essence the highway of the day.

This vessel is the same type of boat as the Senator
Courtesy Steam Boat Times

There appears to be no written account of his trip up the Mississippi River, however many have written about it before and since Rasmus's journey. Samuel Clemens, who coined the name Mark Twain, wrote about the muddy Mississippi River in his immortalized writings of Tom Sawyer and Huckleberry Fin. Clemens himself was a river boat pilot in his younger years. The boats were very popular for travel, from settlement to settlement along the river. In the year 1850, Saint Louis alone, saw close to 3000 arrivals of steamboats. This was just a year after Rasmus passed through there. No two steamboats looked alike, all had a smoke stack on each side of the boat (Port and Starboard), paddle wheels, a pilot house on the upper deck, an engine exhaust and were very poorly built of different woods, canvas, wire, tin and shingles.

The boats hosted elaborate interiors, with grand stair cases, luxurious passenger cabins, food and painted murals, throughout the ship. Entertainment was provided with singing, plenty of alcohol drinking, gambling and women, it's the same today.

The river was treacherous and unpredictable. Over time some 55 boats sank in the river. When the boats would snag on floating debris, like trees or ground on sand bars, the captain would often exercise his authority and cause the crew and passengers to help free her. Sometimes this meant pulling the boat along the rivers edge with ropes. Some captains would keep mules on board for that purpose.

When the boats would make their stops at the settlements along the river, they would blow their steam whistles and draw crowds of spectators. They brought mail, food and trade. There were small settlements that would provide cut wood for the steamers, and some where the captains would beach the boat and stay the night at. The riverboat trade didn't drop off until the Civil War, when boats were restricted from travel on the river. After the Civil War, the Transcontinental Railroad was constructed and became the preferred way of travel.

When the boats lost their luster to fancy rail-road travel, some of them pushed barges up and down the river in order to financially survive. Many of the boats converted their upper deck into an entertainment stage. Entertainment consisted of watching a Shakespeare play, listening to opera, vaudeville acts and burlesque. Rasmus certainly must have enjoyed those future years of boat travel. When the railroad came to Saint Paul, it connected with Chicago and became the place to go. Rasmus traveled there many times and in later years settled their for a long period of time.

Chapter Three

MAKING A NEW LIFE

Rasmus soon arrived at his new home, a small settlement located on the east bank of the Mississippi River, just down river from where the confluence of the Mississippi and Saint Peters Rivers converge, where a frontier outpost known as Fort Snelling, was and still is located.

As the boat docked he stepped off onto a wood planked small dirt embankment. Above the embankment, overlooking the Mississippi River, were dirt cart and wagon roads, lined with small wooden shanty houses, merchant shops, whiskey shops and a log chapel. The inhabitants were made up of Indians, French, French Canadians, Germans, Swedish, Irish, Czech, Hungarians, Polish and Mexicans.

The mixed settlement, was at that time, referred to as the "Town of Saint Paul". It was geographically located a short distance from Saint Anthony Falls. Shortly after Rasmus's arrival, a private firm in Wisconsin measured the town as being 280 acres in size. The population consisted of 910 inhabitants.

In November of 1849, by an act of the Assembly of the Territory of Minnesota, the town received its first official recognition as "Town of Saint Paul". In March of 1854, the name was changed to "City of Saint Paul, Minnesota Territory". In May of 1858, Minnesota became a state and renamed the city as "City of Saint Paul, State of Minnesota".

When Rasmus first arrived in Saint Paul, he noticed that it was a very small, struggling community, in desperate need of commerce trade. The town itself really didn't have anything to offer in the way of trade, and simply existed as a riverboat stop that provided for the needs of whiskey and women for the soldiers stationed at nearby Fort Snelling.

Rasmus answered the towns call for farmers. He homesteaded 40 acres of land of which he farmed. Wheat was the common crop. Later in years, his land would extend to 160 acres. As the farming community grew, Saint Paul's, population, prosperity and trade grew. They now had something to trade with, fresh produce.

On March 29, 1857, Rasmus married Caroline Larson, born December 2, 1839. She later died on October 25, 1905. Sometime during the next two years he traveled, possibly by train, to Illinois. Caroline gave birth to Olive Elizabeth Olson, in Illinois, she was born April 1859 and died August 23, 1939, in the City of Volin, Yankton County, South Dakota, where she is buried. According to a United States Census taken June 10, 1880, Caroline indicated that she gave birth to six children and that only Elizabeth survived. At that time they resided at 276 Halsted Street, Chicago, Ward 13. At one time Rasmus and Caroline residing as in-laws with Elizabeth, residing at #10 Broom Street, Chicago, Illinois. As a foot note, Elizabeth married John Nelson, who fought in the Spanish American War in 1898.

CAROLYN LARSON
RASMUS'S WIFE MARRIED MARCH 29, 1857
Family Album

MARRIAGE LICENSE.

STATE OF ILLINOIS, } ss. The People of the State of Illinois:
LA SALLE COUNTY,

To any regular Minister of the Gospel authorized to marry by the Church or Society to which he belongs, any Justice of the Supreme Court, Judge or Justice of the Peace, SEND GREETING:

Upon Application being made, and it satisfactorily appearing to the Clerk of the county Court of La Salle county, that Rasmus Olson is of the age of Twenty-one Years, and that Caroline Larson is of the age of Eighteen Years,

WE DO GRANT THIS LICENSE, and authorize either of you to solemnize the rite of Marriage between the above named individuals within said county; and we hereby require you to make Certificate of such Marriage and return the same, together with this License, to the Clerk of our said court, within Thirty Days after solemnizing such Marriage.

IN TESTIMONY WHEREOF, The subscriber, Clerk of the County Court of La Salle County, has hereunto set his Hand and affixed the Seal of said Court, at Ottawa, this 27 day of March 1857

Saml W Raymond Clerk
[illegible] Depy

STATE OF ILLINOIS, } ss.
LA SALLE COUNTY,

I DO HEREBY CERTIFY, That by virtue of and pursuant to the authority in the above License granted, I DID, on the 27 day of March 1857 solemnize the Rite of Marriage between Rasmus Olson and Caroline Larson therein named.

Dated this 27 day of March 1857

[illegible]

FREE TRADER PRINT.

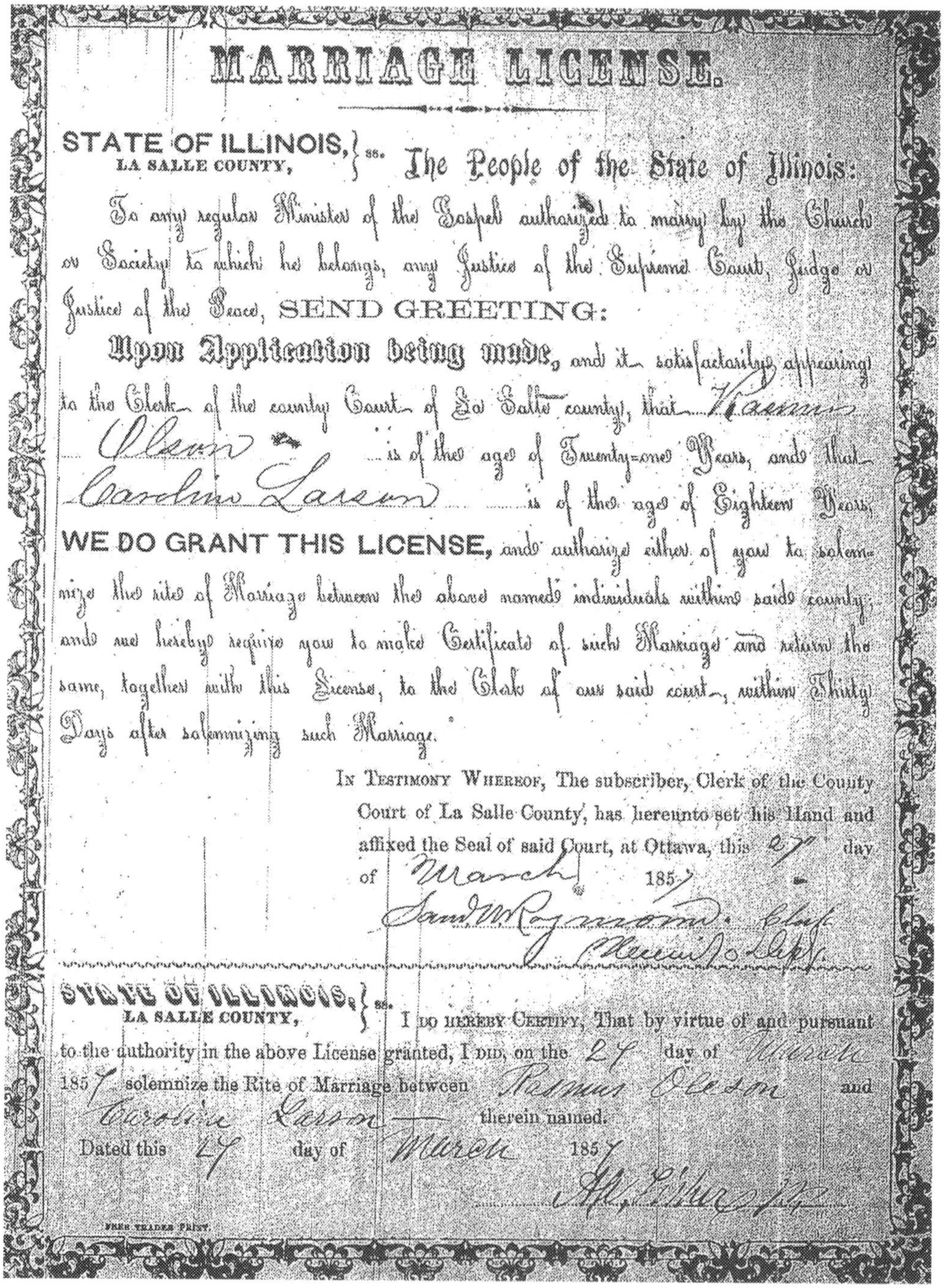

MARRIAGE LICENSE
RASMUS AND CAROLYN CIRCA 1857
FRONT
Family Album

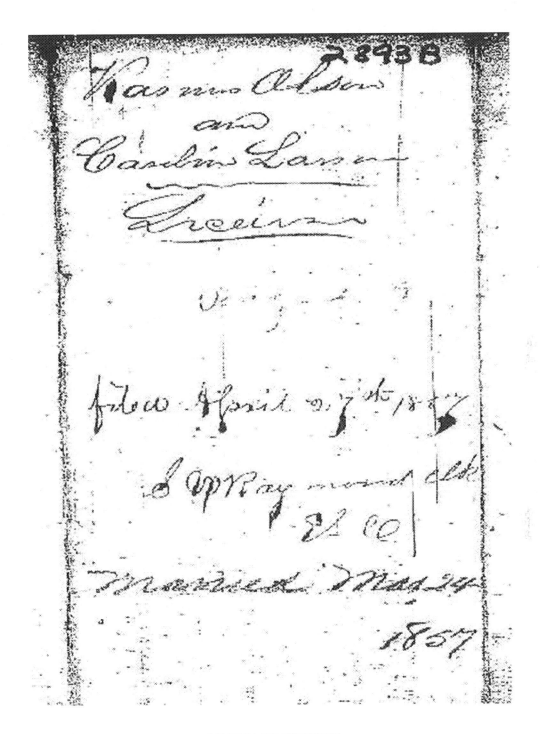

MARRIAGE LICENSE
RASMUS AND CAROLYN CIRCA 1857
BACK SIDE
Family Album

OLIVE ELIZABETH
OLSON
RASMUS'S DAUGHTER
Family Album

JOHN NELSON
OLIVE'S HUSBAND
Family Album

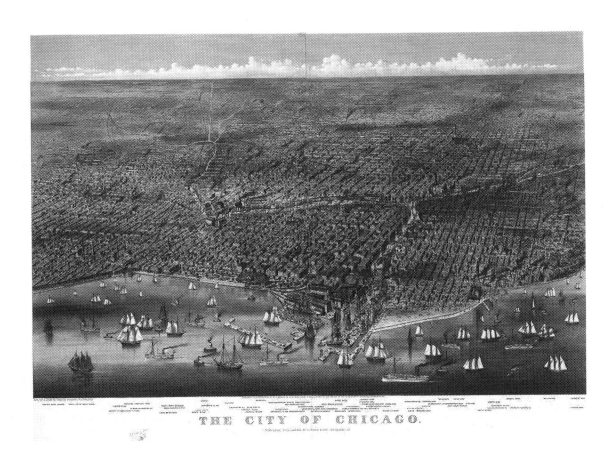

CHICAGO
CIRCA 1880, PAINTER UNKNOWN

Chapter Four

THE DAKOTA INDIAN WARS
The Great Sioux Indian Massacre

As the town grew, other towns sprang up. More and more land was being consumed in order to produce space and food for the new pioneers.

The increase in population meant more needs for land. Like other territories in the United States, those needed lands were simply taken from the Indian's. It wouldn't be long before we encroached on their way of life. In 1851, Minnesota's tribal Dakota Indian's, sold their traditional lands to the U.S. Government, keeping only a small area along the Minnesota River for themselves. To keep the Indians in check, the U.S. Government established the Lower Sioux Agency that administered to their needs.

The Agency acted as a distribution center so that every year the Dakota Indians could receive, from the Agency, money and food, as promised in their land sale. The Agency helped the Indians by having available farming supervisors, teachers and missionaries, who worked to change traditional Dakota life.

Trouble started when the U.S. Government decided to hold back on the monies promised to some 5000 Indians. In addition, they withheld their promised food. The Indians were now facing a cold winter without enough food to feed the tribe. No matter how much the Indians appealed for help, their pleas went unheard. The local trading post, was another outlet for the Indians to trade with and use cash to buy things. Matters were made worst when they began cheating the Indians on their fur trades and raised the cost of food. It didn't take long after that for unrest to start.

The fort put out a call for volunteers in case trouble erupted in the area. Rasmus was one of those who answered their call for help.

On August 11, 1862, some thirteen years after coming to Saint Paul, Rasmus enlisted in the U.S. Army as a Private. He enlisted into the U.S. Army, 6th Regiment of the Minnesota Volunteer Infantry, with Company A, commanded by Captain Hiram P. Grant. He immediately began his training at the famous Northwest outpost, Fort Snelling. Rasmus was older than most of the other recruits, in fact he lied about his age by a two years, saying he was born in 1827, so that he would not be disqualified, due to older age restrictions. Rasmus was a large, tall man, with steely eyes and a commanding presence. It didn't take long for his Commanding Officer to identify his leadership qualities and promote him to the rank of Corporal. Back in the early days of the Army, if you showed no fear and stood up for yourself, and were good with your hands in a fight, you were considered valuable in controlling those who may be a problem. Those qualities are what was needed to keep the other recruits in line. That same theory applies today when the recruits are terrorized by their drill instructor. That is done on purpose. To promote discipline in combat.

On August 19, 1862, the Santee Sioux Indians, led by Chief Little Crow, went on the offensive. They were very angry over what was happening to them, the loss of their lands, way of life and the U.S. Governments failure to provide for them as they had agreed to in a treaty. The Indians began there offensive by going into the settlement and killing over 800 inhabitants. At the same time, just twelve miles north of then town of New Ulm, also then under attack, seventy three soldiers at Redwood Ferry, were caught off guard, by the attacking Indians. Twenty three soldiers were killed in that skirmish.

During these raids, the Indians took more than 300 women and children as prisoners. Many homesteads were burned to the ground, food storages were looted and livestock was taken. The raiding parties had little or no mercy. The settlers down river took refuge at another Northwest outpost, Fort Ridgely, which still stands today as does Fort Snelling. Fort Ridgely was not designed for defense. It was a storage place for goods and supplies and was occupied by both soldiers and refugees.

RASMUS OLSON MILITARY SERVICE FILE
Courtesy of National Archives

FORT SNELLING

LOCATION ON MISSISSIPPI RIVER OF
FORT SNELLING
Courtesy of My Genealogist.com

Chapter Five

AUGUST 20-22, 1862

BATTLE AT FORT RIDGELY

A few days later Fort Ridgley came under attack by an estimated 1000 Sioux Indians. Unlike other frontier forts, Fort Ridgely did not have a wall surrounding it. It was spread out over a large compound on a small flat hill. The soldiers defended the fort, took up firing positions from inside the granite rock faced structures that housed their barracks and administrative buildings.

A deep ravine close by, provided refuge and an assembly point for the Indians. The trench or coolie as they are sometimes called in that part of the country, ran north and south on the east side of the fort, which gave the Indians cover and concealment.

During the ensuing battle, an artillery Sergeant took up a position at one of the buildings and was credited with saving the fort through his rapid cannon exchange against the Indians. Some of the Indians overtook buildings and used them to fire on the other soldiers. The artillery Sergeant fired directly at the buildings, destroying them and killing the Indians inside. A volunteer soldier snuck through the enemy lines and managed to reach Fort Snelling.

On August 24, 1862, Colonel H. Sibley, immediately dispatched nine companies of troops to come to the aid of Fort Ridgely. All of the soldiers were untrained and none were experienced in combat. Rasmus was dispatched with Company A and took part in this event. Colonel Sibley's troops made a forced march, arriving on August 28. Upon arrival of Sibley's troops, an enemy engagement pursued and the Indians fled back into the nearby forest areas. After action reports indicated that if it were not for the cannon fire from Ordinance Sergeant John Jones the Fort may have fallen before the relief troops arrived.

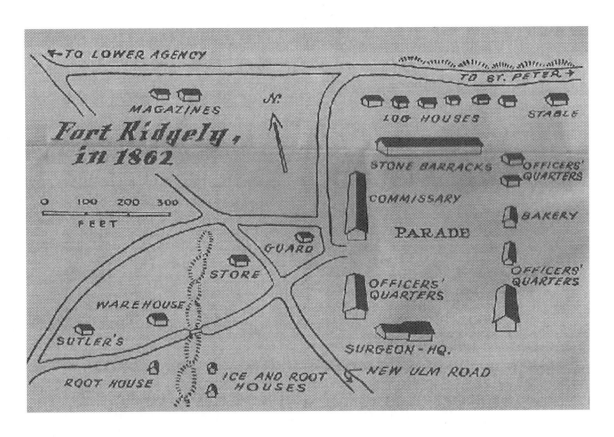

Drawing courtesy of Minnesota Historical Society

Photo's by Author

FORT RIDGELY   ACTUAL ORIGINAL BUILDING

MODEL OF FORT RIDGELY

This was the first time that Rasmus saw combat. I found that in my research, some of the adventures that Rasmus had, I also experienced. As example, on March 13, 1967, I was awarded the Bronze Star Medal for valor, while coming to the relief of a South Vietnamese outpost (fort) in the Mekong Delta, Vietnam. He helped save a fort from the enemy and I, his Great-Great Grandson, helped save a fort from the enemy.

Photo by Author

FARMING LAND THAT SURROUNDS BIRCH COULEE
Photo by Author

Courtesy of Fort Ridgely Museum

BRIGADIER GENERAL HENRY HASTINGS SIBLEY
Circa 1862 courtesy of Minnesota Historical Society

"You are fools. You cannot see the face of your Chief; your eyes are full of smoke. You cannot hear his voice; your ears are full of roaring waters. Braves, you are little children—you are fools. You will die like the rabbits when the hungry wolves hunt them in the hard moon (January). Taoyateduta is not a coward: He will die with you."

CHIEF LITTLE CROW
Taoyateduta
Photo Courtesy of Smithsonian Institution

"We felt the fort was the door to the valley, but the soldiers kept the door shut." Wamditanka (Big Eagle) Mdewakanton Leader

CHIEF BIG EAGLE
Photo Courtesy of Smithsonian Institution

REPRODUCTION OF THE MEDAL RASMUS RECEIVED BY THE
STATE OF MINNESOTA FOR HIS INVOLVEMENT IN THE RES-
CUE OF FORT RIDGELY

Chapter Six

SEPTEMBER 1-3, 1862

BATTLE AT BIRCH COULEE

On August 30, 1862, Colonel H. H. Sibley, of the sixth Minnesota Infantry, detailed Company "A" (*Rasmus's Company*), under command of Captain Hiram P. Grant, to scout the countryside for hostile Indians, to round up any survivors, and to bury the fallen soldiers at Redwood Ferry. The expedition was also charged with searching for and burying any inhabitants that were killed.

The expedition consisted of Captain Grants Company, some Calvary under Captain Anderson, some Renville Ranger scouts and a few citizens. There also was a detail of 20 men to act as a burial party. In all there was 150 men. Each man was issued 40 rounds of ammunition and two days provisions. An extra 3000 rounds of ammunition was also provided in case it was needed.

They had been in the field two days and buried 80 individuals. No Indians were found at the Lower Sioux Agency. Sometime before dark, the soldiers made camp, located in a high flat grass area, near a good flowing stream of water which was surrounded by birch trees.

This area was known to the local inhabitants as "Birch Coulee". The word "coulee" is French and denotes a stream with steep banks. The company assembled themselves into a wagon circle, like you would see in an old John Wayne movie.

The unit consisted of 20 horse drawn wagons, which were placed in the form of a horseshoe, end to end, enclosing a space of about one half acre. Picket guards were sent out a little ways from the encampment, tents were assembled and the horses were corralled on a rope. Joseph R. Brown, who held the title of Major from having been an Indian Agent, went with the party. Major Browns family, of part Indian blood, were prisoners with the Indians.

He was anxious to learn something of his family and it was believed that his advice would be of value to Captain Grant. Because of this, he was part of the Expedition, however, Captain Grant was in charge. No preparation for defense was taken to protect the camp in the event of an attack. This was because Major Brown convinced the other officers that the Indians would not attack them. Robert K. Boyd, a survivor of the battle wrote; *"Major Brown did not think there were any Indians in that vicinity, and at this camped the men that they were just as safe as if they were in there own homes"*.

No one felt different about that, because they had all been in the service a couple of weeks, and in fact they were so green that almost none of the men were yet trained in how to fire the service rifle.

The men were totally exhausted from riding and burying settlers. They had been out for two days, away from any comforts that the fort had to offer.

At approximately 4:00 a.m., one of the sentries spotted something moving in the grass, heading towards the sleeping troops. Realizing that it was an Indian, he immediately opened fire and killed the Indian. At the exact same moment that the sentry fired at the Indian, some 800 Sioux Indians who had silently surrounded the encampment through the night, opened fire on the troops.

Almost immediately, all 94 horses tied up on the East side of the camp were killed by arrows and rifle shots. Several soldiers fell mortally wounded, and many more lay wounded. This occurred in the first two minutes of fighting.

There was no place to seek cover or concealment from the hail of bullets and arrows, and according to after actions reports, the soldiers piled there dead comrades on top of the dead horses and fired from those positions. Aside from shooting from behind the wagons, there simply was no other place to protect yourself.

Robert Boyd wrote *"It may be said that a murderous fire was kept up all day, and all night, there was an occasionally volley".*

The battle raged on for 32 hours. The troops were low on ammunition, water and had no food during that time. The expedition suffered almost fifty percent casualties. Colonel Sibley dispatched troops to help, however those troops found themselves pinned down by the Indians. Cannon fire from that relief column was heard back at Fort Ridgeley. Hearing this Colonel Sibley dispatched his full force. arriving at Birch Cooley around noon time on that second day. Seeing this the Indians broke off the fight and left.

Rasmus was one of the 50 men wounded during the fight. His wounds were later treated by the Regiment's Assistant Surgeon, Doctor Daniels. It is not know how, by what or where Rasmus was wounded. His name on the battlefield monument attests to being one of the wounded.

On September 3, 1862, Rasmus, through his actions on the battle field, was battlefield promoted to the rank of Sergeant. When the battle ended the dead were buried and the wounded cared for.

On June 13, 2003, almost 150 years later, while researching my family roots, I walked alone in the evening hours, upon that very same battlefield. I could feel the plight of those poor soldiers. They had absolutely no trees, trenches or anything for cover, except their wagons, dead horses and dead fellow soldiers. As you walk down a special trail on the battlefield, signs point out as to the directions that the Indians attacked from and a host of history about the battle. I equated my experiences in Vietnam and became as one with the battlefield. I could feel the struggle and my military training and experience allowed me to visualize the soldiers tactical movements and situation. In today's terms, the soldiers were a target rich environment for the Indians. My personal evaluation of the soldiers camp site was that it was not good. The soldiers needed to camp in and around the birch tree coulee.

If they had done that, it would have afforded them proper cover and concealment. Additionally, a fresh water stream would have passed through the camp, that would provide water for drinking, cooking, washing and cleansing of wounds.

The trees would have afforded the troops protective firing points or positions, and made it near impossible for the Indians to penetrate their flanks. The ditch, in itself would have harbored the units 94 horses and kept them from harm or capture. The coulee would have been a relatively safe medical evacuation point and would better protect the units surgeon during the care of the wounded, while he was under fire. Entrenchment in the coulee would have also provided a functional location for a command center or post.

Additionally, the natural geographical placement of the trench to the open prairie, where the troops actually camped in the open, would have easily accommodated listening posts and right and left flanking positions. The wagons would have been better off positioned parallel to the trench to provide additional fortification and easy access to ammunition and supplies. In my opinion, the Indians would have never attacked that type of entrenchment. The Indians were better at soldering than we gave them credit for. These very same Indians, fourteen years later, wiped out General George Armstrong Custer's Seventh Calvary at the Battle of Little Big Horn.

ACTUAL PHOTOGRAPH OF SETTLERS ON THE PRAIRIE
HIDING FROM THE INDIANS
COURTESY MINNESOTA HISTORICAL SOCIETY
CIRCA 1862

BATTLE OF BIRCH COULEE
COURTESY MINNESOTA HISTORICAL SOCIETY

Looking from Soldiers Camp
towards Direction of Attack

INDIAN POSITIONS

COMPANY A CAMPED HERE

Photo's by Author

Photo's by Author

BIRCH COULEE
BATTLEFIELD
SEPTEMBER 2, 1862
ADMINISTERED BY MINN HISTORICAL SOCIETY

Company A camped here

Indians attacked from these positions

BIRCH COULEE BATTLEFIELD

BIRCH COULEE CREEK

THIS IS WHERE THE INDIANS ATTACKED FROM. PHOTO
TAKEN BY AUTHOR FROM A SMALL BRIDGE CROSSING, AT
THE BATTLEFIELD SITE.

Photo by Author

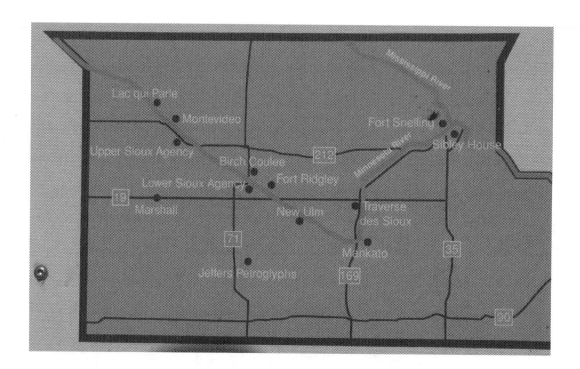

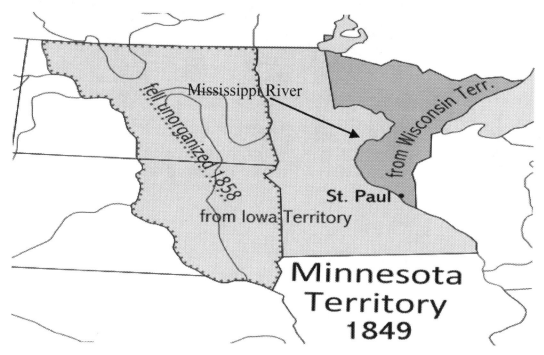

Courtesy of Wikimedia Commons

BATTLE OF BIRCH COULEE

Painted by Dorothea Paul

Courtesy of Minnesota Historical Society
By A.P. Connolly

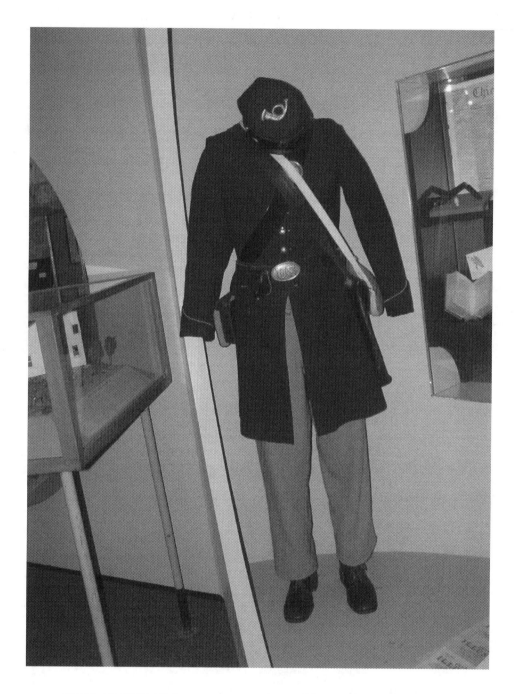

THIS IS THE TYPE OF UNIFORM THAT RASMUS WORE
Photo taken by author at Fort Ridgely Museum

Pencil rub made by author on battlefield monument

Birch Coulee Battlefield Monument
Erected 1899 Morton, Minnesota

Engraved on this Monument
Humanity, Patriotism Courage and Fidelity

FORT RIDGELY MONUMENT
ON THIS BATTLEFIELD MONUMENT
STANDS THE ENGRAVED NAME OF RASMUS OLSON

Chapter Seven

SEPTEMBER 23, 1862

BATTLE AT WOOD LAKE

On September 19, 1862, A large contingent of soldiers left Fort Ridgley, under the command of newly promoted General Henry H. H. Sibley. Rasmus's Company "A", was a part of that contingent of soldiers. The following is quoted from Official Reports and Correspondence by General Sibley, written at Wood Lake, Yellow Medicine, Minnesota.

"SIR: I left the camp at Fort Ridgley on the 19th instant with my command and reached this point early in the afternoon of the 22nd instant. There have been small parties of Indians each day in plain sight, evidently acting as scouts for the main body. This morning I had determined to cross the Yellow Medicine river, about three miles distant, and there await.

The arrival of Captain Rogers' company of the Seventh Regiment, which was ordered by me from New Ulm to join me by a forced march, the presence of the company there being necessary by the arrival of another company a few days previously. About 7 o'clock this morning the camp was attacked by about 300 Indians, who suddenly made there appearance and dashed down towards us whooping and yelling in their usual style and firing with great rapidity. The Renville Guards under Lieutenant Gorman, was sent by me to check them, and Major Welch, of the Third Regiment, was instantly in line with his command, his skirmishes in the advance, by whom the savages were gallantly met and, after a conflict of a serious nature, repulsed. Meantime another portion of the Indian force passed down a ravine, with a view to out-flank the Third Regiment, and I ordered Lieutenant Colonel Marshall, with five companies of the Seventh Regiment, who was ably seconded by Major Bradley, to advance, to its support with one 6-pounder, under the command of Captain Hendricks, and I also ordered two companies of the Sixth Regiment to reinforce him. Lieutenant Colonel Marshal advanced amid a shower of balls from the enemy, which fortunately did little damage and cleared the ravine of the savages. Major Mc Laren, with Captain Wilson's Company, took position on the extreme left of the camp, where he kept at bay a party of the enemy who were endeavoring to gain the rear of the camp and finally drove them back. The battle raged for about two hours, the 6-pounder and the mountain howitzer being used with great effect, when the Indians, repulsed at all points with great loss, retired with precipitation.

I regret to state that many casualties occurred on our side. The gallant Major Welch was badly wounded in the leg and Captain Wilson, of the Sixth, was severely bruised by a nearby spent ball in the shoulder. Four of our men were killed, and between 35 and 40 were wounded, most of them, I rejoice to hear, not seriously. The loss of the enemy, according to the statement of a half-breed named Joseph Campbell, who visited the camp under a flag of truce, was 30 killed and a large number wounded. We found and buried 14 of the bodies, and, as the habit of the Indians is to carry off the bodies of their slain, it is not probable that the sum total as given by Campbell was exaggerated.

The severe chastisement inflicted upon them has so far subdued their arbor that they sent a flag of truce into my camp to express the sentiments of the Wahpetons, a part of the attacking force, and to state that they were not strong enough to fight us; that they desired peace, with the permission to take away their dead and wounded. To this I replied that when the prisoners held by them were delivered up there would be time enough to talk of peace, and that I would not give them permission either to take their dead or wounded. I am assured by Campbell that there is serious dissension in the Indian camp, many having been opposed to the war, but driven into the field by the more violent. He further states that 800 men were assembled at the Yellow Medicine, within two miles of my camp, but that the greater part took no *share in the fight. The Intention of Little Crow was to attack us last night, but he was overruled by others, who told him if he was a brave man he ought to fight the white man by daylight.*

I am fully prepared against a night attack should it be attempted, although I think the lesson I received by them today will make them very cautious in the future.

I have already adverted to the courage and skill of Lieutenant Colonel Marshall and Majors Welch and Bradley, to which I beg leave to add those of the officers and men of their respective commands. Lieutenant Colonel Averill and Major Mc Laren were equally prompt in there movements in preparing the Sixth Regiment for action, and were both under fire for some time. Captains Grant (Rasmus's Captain) and Bromley shared the dangers of the field with Lieutenant Colonel Marshall's command, while Captain Wilson, with his company rendered essential service. The other companies of the Sixth Regiment were not engaged, having been held in position to defend the rear of the camp, but it was difficult to restrain their arbor, so anxious were officers and men to share with their comrades the perils of the field. To Lieutenant Colonel Fowler, my Assistant Adjutant General, I have been greatly indebted for aid in all my movements, his military knowledge and ability being invaluable to me, and his assistance in today's affair particularly so. To Major Forbes, Messrs, Patch, Greig, and Mc Keod of my staff, who carried my orders, I must also acknowledge myself under obligations for their activity and zeal; while to Major Brown, also my staff, although suffering from illness, it would be injustice not to state that he aided me materially. The medical staff of the several regiments were cool and expert in rendering their professional aid to the wounded. Assistant Surgeon Seigneuret, attached to my staff, is to be commended for his skill and diligence.

I am very much in want of bread rations, 6-pounder ammunition, and shells for the howitzer; and unless soon supplied I shall be obligated to fall back, which under present circumstances would be a calamity, as it would afford time for the escape of the Indians with their captives. I hope a large body of cavalry is before this on their way to join me. If I had been provided with 500 of this description of force today I venture the assertion that I could have killed the greater portion of the Indians and brought the Campaign to a successful close. Rev. Mr. Riggs, Chaplain of the expedition, so well known for his knowledge of the character and language of the Indians, has been of the greatest service to me since he joined my command.

I enclose the official report of Lieutenant Colonel Marshall. I omitted to mention Lieutenant Gorman and his corps of Renville Rangers. They have been extremely useful to me by their courage and skill as skirmishers. Captain Hendricks and his artillerists won deserved praise today, and Captain Sterrett, with his small but gallant cavalry, only 27 in number, did good service also.

Very respectfully, your obedient servant,

H.H. Sibley
Colonel, Commanding

His Excellency, ALEXANDER RAMSEY,

[Explanatory Note]
St. Paul, Minn., Nov. 18, 1865

The foregoing dispatch was addressed to the Governor of Minnesota, under whose authority I was Acting as Colonel commanding the expeditionary forces against the hostile Sioux Indians. Major General Pope had been assigned to the general command in the Department of the Northwest prior to the battle of Wood Lake, but I had not yet received the order requiring me to report to him which reached me subsequently.

H.H. Sibley
Brigadier General U.S. Volunteers"

The above quotations are of factual record and serve to better explain the battle as it unfolded. Further Official Reports and Correspondence from Lieutenant Colonel Marshall firmly places Rasmus's company in the thick of this battle.

"Report of Lieut. Col. William R. Marshall, Seventh Minnesota Infantry

HEADQUARTERS SEVENTH REGIMENT MINNESOTA VOLUNTEERS,
CAMP AT WOOD LAKE MINN., Sept. 23, 1862

Colonel: I have the honor to submit the following report of the Seventh Regiment (five companies) in the engagement with the Indians this morning. Immediately after the first alarm was given the men were formed on company grounds to await orders. These soon came, and the battalion marched to the support of the gun (6-pounder) served by Captain Hendricks on the right, on North side of camp. Captain Gilfillan, with Company H, of the Seventh, was on guard. He was ordered to place half his men in the rifle-pits (dug for the protection of camp), and to advance the others as skirmishers on the extreme right. I lengthened my line to the right of the gun, and somewhat in advance, facing the ravine occupied by the Indians. Gradually advancing the line, the men keeping close to the ground and firing as they crawled forward, I gained a good position from which to charge the Indians. Leaving two companies with the gun I pursued with the rest beyond the ravine until recalled by your order.

The following are the casualties in my command: Private Charles Frink, Company A, killed; Sergt. C. C. Chapman, Company B, wounded by gun-shot, in the wrist; Private Charles Billings, Company B, wounded by gunshot in the thigh; Private John Ober, Company G, bruised in foot by a spent ball.

Shortly after our return to camp we were ordered out to prevent the Indians recovering the bodies of their dead in the ravine. With Captain Hendricks' gun again advanced to the edge of the ravine, we gathered up 6 bodies, which with 1 brought in before, made 7 of the enemy's dead brought in by my command. All, both officers and men, behaved admirably; commands were promptly obeyed; not a man flinched under fire. Captain Hendricks and men under my immediate notice, if not strictly under my command, behaved handsomely.

Very respectfully, your obedient servant,

Wm. R. Marshall
Lieutenant Colonel, Comdg. Seventh Regt. Minn. Vols.
Col. H. H. Sibley,
Commanding Indian Expedition.

55

Note.-There was in this action Companies A,B,F,G, and H, all of the regiment that was in this expedition."

AUTHOR'S NOTE

The Battle of Wood Lake actually occurred at Lone Tree Lake. Wood Lake is three and a half miles west of Lone Tree Lake. The soldiers thought that they were at Wood Lake and so recorded it as that.

Chapter Eight

FRONTIER DUTY

Following the Union victory at Wood Lake, Rasmus and his company returned to Fort Ridgely where he remained on frontier duty, scouting for Indians and protecting the area inhabitants, until September of 1862. On September 26, 1862, he mustered in at Camp Release, located in Lac qui parle County, Minnesota. Camp Release is known today as Camp Release Township. It is as far west as you can go, in southern Minnesota and boarders the state of South Dakota. Sometime in early November 1862, his unit left Camp Release and traveled to Fort Snelling, where he did garrison duty until February 1863.

Garrison duty was, to a soldier, boring.

When a soldier was in the field, on patrol, life was exciting and trivial tasks, for the most part, were nonexistent. Your superiors weren't concerned about the shine on your boots or the length of your hair. Scouting and stalking the enemy brought an excitement that one could not get through garrison duty. If one was lucky, part of his garrison duty would include mounting your horse and running errands, like carrying messages back and forth between forts and other military posts. It gave you a chance to be free in the great outdoors and pass and receive news of home.

A typical day on garrison duty would be something like this; wake up at 5:30 a.m., make your bed and clean your area, shave, wash and put your uniform on. At 6:00 a.m. you would have your mess kit in hand and be standing in line at the mess hall. After eating, you would have time to organize your equipment. At 7:30 a.m. you would muster on the grinder or parade area. There you would be inspected by the Platoon Sergeant to make sure that you were not drunk and that your uniform was up to standards.

The Commanding Officer wound then disseminate information about the war, about the intentions of what your company or platoon will be doing that day, what he expects of you, messages that just came in from the Department of the Army or the Commanding General, and a host of other directives. Following the address from the Commanding Officer, your Platoon Sergeant would then hand out individual assignments for the day. Those assignments may include digging earth works to protect the fort, cooking details, guard duty assignments, feeding and care for the horses, clean up details like cleaning the barracks, working in the administrative office, cleaning of the cannon, wheel packing of grease on the wagon wheels, guarding a work detail of prisoners and disciplined troops, building other structures like buildings and walls or repairing same, orderly duty to the officers, making bullets by hand, loading and unloading supply wagons, clearing trees and brush from the fort perimeter and a host of other activities.

Following dismissal from the ranks, you would proceed to your duty assignment. At 12:00 p.m., you would again find yourself standing in line for lunch or as they called it your noon meal. Lunch would usually last an hour. At 1:00 p.m. you would again muster with the unit for roll call and for receipt of new information or orders. From about 2:00 p.m. until 5:00 p.m., you would normally be in training, either as an individual with your squad, platoon, the battalion or the regiment. Training may have included troop movements, battle tactics, rifle and pistol target shooting, horsemanship, sword fighting, marching, personal hygiene, cleaning of your sword or firearm as well as other forms of military duties. A famous pastime would include gambling, story telling or drinking. Drinking of alcoholic beverages was not allowed, however it was often over-looked, especially if you have just come in from patrol or had an engagement with the enemy.

INDIAN WAR BATTLE

1862-1864

MAPS

ONTARIO CANADA

BATTLE OF BIRCH COULEE

(MORTON, MN)

WISCONSIN

NORTH DAKOTA

SOUTH DAKOTA

CAMP RELEASE

MINNESOTA RIVER

SAINT PAUL

FORT SNELLING

MISSOURI RIVER

FORT RIDGELY

TO SAINT LOUIS

BATTLE OF WOOD LAKE

LOWER SIOUX AGENCY INDIAN CAMP

IOWA

GLENCO MILITARY POST

COUNTY MAP OF THE STATE OF MINNESOTA
SHOWING MAJOR SITES OF IMPORTANCE

NORTH DAKOTA INDIAN BATTLES THAT RASMUS FOUGHT

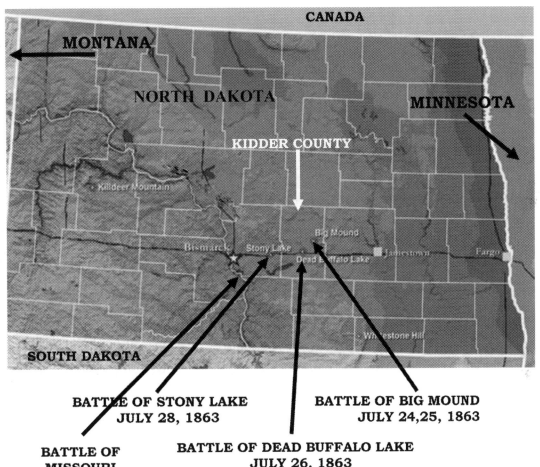

BATTLE OF STONY LAKE
JULY 28, 1863

BATTLE OF BIG MOUND
JULY 24,25, 1863

BATTLE OF
MISSOURI
JULY 29,30,1863

BATTLE OF DEAD BUFFALO LAKE
JULY 26, 1863

AUTHOR'S NOTE

THE DAKOTA SIOUX THAT GENERAL SIBLEY AND RASMUS'S COMPANY "A", UNDER CAPTAIN GRANT, CHASED AND SKIRMISHED WITH, CLEAR ACROSS MINNESOTA AND THEN ON INTO NORTH DAKOTA, LATER JOINED UP WITH THE CHEYENNE TRIBE. ON JUNE 25, 26, 1876, 13 YEARS LATER, ATTACKED AND KILLED LIEUTENANT COLONEL GEORGE A. CUSTER AND HIS 7TH CAVALRY DETACHMENT AT THE BATTLE OF LITTLE BIG HORN IN MONTANA.

Chapter Nine

July 24, 1863

BATTLE AT BIG MOUND

On July 24, 1863, Company "A", attached to General Henry H. H. Sibley had been chasing the Sioux Indians for days, only catching a glimpse of their scouts from time to time. The Santee and Teton Sioux Indian tribes had united in a show of strength.

On the day of the battle, General Sibley ordered the troops to break camp and mount up. They marched southwest across an area known as the Missouri Hills of Coteau. As was the standard operating practice in those days, the Army would send out scouts ahead of the column. The scouts would report back and forth to the General and advise him on travel routes so that wagons could pass safely.

The scouts however had other important and functional responsibilities. They stalked Indian movements and would report back to the Commanding General giving the enemy strength, location and direction of travel. They also would locate and recommend places to pitch camp, usually near a source of water, which had good concealment, and one that has a defendable position. Scouts were often paid civilians with an extensive knowledge of the area and the Indians, or they were friendly Indians.

Around noon time, they reported back to General Sibley and advised him that they had found the Indians that he had been chasing, since Minnesota.

The column marched up onto a plateau and from there began moving down into a small valley. As they started down into the valley they observed Indians off to the East, the South and to the West. By now Sibley's troops needed rest before engaging the hostile Indians. The bewildered troops needed to be fed, along with their horses' and the men needed rest. The place that they set up camp was later named Camp Sibley.

The General ordered that the camp immediately set up it's defenses. This meant that guards or sentries had to take up strategic positions to be able to alert the Regiment in case of attack. Trenches had to be dug and breastworks (temporary fortification) made. The scouts took us positions some 400 yards from the main camp. The Indians were well aware that the troops were there. They were approached by the Dakota, who asked to parley with General Sibley.

Doctor Josiah S. Weiser, Chief Surgeon to the accompanying unit, 1st Regiment of the Minnesota Mounted Rangers, could talk Dakota. During the discussion he was shot and killed by three of the Indians sent to parley. Both parties took cover and ex-changed gun fire, while seeking defensible positions. The barrage of gunfire alerted troops setting up camp and they formed into battle lines. Heavy fighting broke out in a large ravine running from the top of the plateau down to the camp. Sibley realized the challenges of fighting the Indians in the ravine and decided to move to higher ground. The troops moved up hill bringing with them a battery of 6 pound field cannons (measured by the weight of the ball shot). The General set up a new command post. The cannons were positioned at higher levels and fired into the ravine killing the Indians that were concealed there. Between the artillery and the advancing troops, the Indians fled.

On the East side of the hill, the 6th Minnesota Volunteers (Rasmus's Regiment) was advancing up hill against lighter opposition. When they fought their way to the top of the bluff they turned south driving the Santee and Teton Indians before them. On the West side, Mc Phail's Ranger's circled West out of camp Sibley, cutting off attack from the exposed side of the camp. The Calvary set up a position South, blockading the Indians from slipping off the plateau to the West. They then wheeled to the right, sandwiching the Indians between themselves and Mc Phail's Rangers. The party of Indians were killed, however the larger band escaped. Following the battle, the General moved the camp about four miles and rested his men until the next day.

DAKOTA SIOUX RAIDING PARTY AND CAMP CIRCA 1863

Courtesy of National Achieves

SIBLEY PURSUING INDIANS AFTER
BIG MOUND INDIAN BATTLE JULY 24, 25, 1863
SKETCH COURTESY OF HARPERS WEEKLY, IT WAS DRAWN ON SITE

SIBLEY PURSUING INDIANS AFTER
BIG MOUND INDIAN BATTLE JULY 24, 25, 1863
SKETCH COURTESY OF HARPERS WEEKLY, IT WAS DRAWN ON SITE

A SIOUX WARRIOR 1863
COURTESY HARPER'S WEEKLY
JULY 26, 1863

Chapter Ten

BATTLE AT DEAD BUFFALO LAKE

On the morning of the 26th, the next day after the Battle of Big Mound, the troops broke camp and marched west about fourteen miles. Early in the morning they passed the Indian's abandoned camp. About noon time they located the Indians, and were ready for them.

At first the fighting was long distance and gradually closed. It seemed that the Indians were not wanting to close the distance between them. A group of the Indians attempted to flank the camps left side and run off the mules and route the livestock. The heavy fighting between the mounted rangers and the infantry soon discouraged the Indians from their intentions.

Following this setback the Indians retreated, ending the battle. General Sibley pursued them. The Sioux were on the run. That night General Sibley ordered that earthworks be thrown up in the event of an attack. There was no attack.

The Indians were using these attacks on the troops in hopes to delay or stall the troops from moving forward. This was done as a tactic because their old, their women and their children were in exodus ahead of them, on their westward advance to escape the pursuing troops.

It isn't known how many Indians were killed in this battle but reports put the army's casualty rate as seven dead and fifteen wounded. There is little more historical information regarding this battle. We do know that Company "A" performed honorably and without blemish.

Chapter Eleven

JULY 28, 1863

BATTLE AT STONY LAKE

Following the Battle of Dead Buffalo Lake, General Sibley again pursued the Indians. Soon it became evident that he had to stop. His horses and mules were exhausted and needed rest. Camp was set. General Sibley soon learned that a large contingent of Indians were moving towards him. He ordered breast works be set in place and ordered his infantry to advance towards the Indians. The Indians were again attempting to slow the advance of the soldiers but it didn't work. The Indians made an effort to find weak places in the soldiers camp and rank. Finding none they ran off at such great speed that they couldn't be chased and engaged. General Sibley would later write that battle at Stony Lake was *"the greatest conflict between our troops and the Indians, so far as the numbers were concerned"*. It is not known how many Indians were in this engagement, however, General Sibley commanded a force of 3000 troops. It has been estimated that the Indian force numbered 2000, having been reinforced from friends on the west side of the Missouri.

In a narrative of the Indian War of 1862-1864, Charles Eugene Flandrau wrote; *"Colonel Baker was directed to deploy two companies as skirmishers and the rest of the command was immediately placed in line, with Colonel Crooks and the Sixth* (Rasmus's Regiment) *on the right, and Colonel Marshall with the Seventh and Mc Phail's cavalry on the left. A tremendous effort was made to break our lines, but the enemy was repulsed at all points. Colonel*

Baker with the Tenth, bore the brunt of the fight, being in advance, where the assault was most furious and determined. The artillery did good work, but the Indians finally retreated and fled in a panic and route towards the Missouri River. They were hotly pursued".

Chapter Twelve

JULY 29, 1863

BATTLE AT MISSOURI RIVER

Following the Battle of Stony Lake, the Indians continued their retreat westward with General Sibley's troops in hot pursuit. On July 29th, 1863, General Sibley's troops crossed Apple Creek, a small stream just a few miles from present day Bismarck, the capitol of North Dakota. Continuing to move westward the troops came to the Missouri River, at a point about four miles above Burt Boat Island.

The Indians had succeeded in crossing the river with their families. They were however demoralized from lack of food, supplies and equipage. When General Sibley reached the opposite shore of the river he could plainly see the Indians on the bluff on the other side.

It was here that Lieutenant Beever lost his life while carrying an order; he had missed the trail, and was ambushed and killed. Lieutenant Beever was a very rich Englishman, who volunteered to accompany the expedition as a member of General Sibley's staff. The bodies of Lieutenant Beever and a Private from the Sixth Regiment, who was killed in the same way, were later recovered and buried.

During the flight the Indians were forced to leave everything they owned behind, that would pose a burden or slow them up during the river crossing. General Sibley found large quantities of wagons and other matcrials left behind. The General ordered Company "A" (Rasmus), Company "I" and Company "K" to destroy all of it, so as to deny the Indians any further use of them.

On July 31, 1863, the order was given by General Sibley to prepare for the march home. On August 1, 1863, the soldiers broke camp and at 5:30 a.m. the order was given to march homeward.

During the Indian Expedition of 1863, Rasmus endured incredible hardships. He marched over 1200 miles, that's like walking half way across the United States, he fought in three well contested battles and was part of an armed force that chased 8,000 to 10,000 Dakota Sioux Indians, clear across and out of the State of Minnesota, and well into the State of North Dakota. Following the expedition the Sixth returned to Camp Release, where they remained on frontier duty until May of 1864. In May The Sixth Regiment departed for Fort Snelling, except for Company "A", "E" and Company "H", who were ordered to report to Fort Ridgley. Shortly after arriving at Fort Ridgley new orders were issued to Rasmus's company. On June 2, 1864, Rasmus's company along with Company "E", were ordered to report to Fort Snelling, to scout for Indians by way of Henderson, Belle Plaine and Shokopee. Having done that without any reportable incidents, he arrived at Fort Snelling, on June 7, 1864, and set camp, at Camp Crooks, which was located one mile above Fort Snelling.

Chapter Thirteen

JUNE 14, 1864

THE AMERICAN CIVIL WAR

Rasmus and his combat distinguished Sixth Minnesota Regiment, were activated by President Abraham Lincoln and Secretary Stanton, and ordered on May 26, 1864, by the War Department, to turn over their frontier duties to another unit and to enter the Civil War as federalized troops.

On June 14, 1864, the Sixth Regiment marched to Saint Paul where Rasmus (Company "A") embarked on the steamboat Enterprise. Other units of the Regiment also embarked on his boat while others embarked on the steamboat Hudson. Each of the boats towed two barges to accompany the troops.

The boats were packed with horses, mules, wagons, men and equipment. They departed at midnight and arrived in Dunleith, Illinois on the 17th. The Regiment then boarded rail road cars and traveled to Cairo (Illinois Central Express), arriving there on the 19th. Rasmus then embarked on the steam-boat Empress and proceeded to Helena, Arkansas. Immediately upon arrival on the 23rd, they set up camp on the river bank, located about one half mile above the town. For the first time shelter tents were issued and were warmly welcomed according to accounts. They called their camp, Camp Buford. The unit had traveled some 1000 miles on the Mississippi River.

The entire Regiment was attached to the District of Eastern Arkansas, 7th Army Corps, Department of Arkansas.

They were assigned duties in Helena that ranged from picket guards to guarding prisoners of war. In the first week of July, orders were issued to build quarters.

The already fatigued, heat struck troops, some of which were sick and many died of disease, began cutting, hauling and sawing wood. This soon stopped because of the general health of the troops. Some of the sickened troops were sent north because of the disease problem.

On the 26th of July, the regiment went out about two miles beyond the picket lines on the Little Rock Road, to cover the retreat of Calvary and colored troops, who that morning in a creek some few miles west of town, had a severe enemy engagement.

On August 1st, believing that an attack on the Union force defenses was immanent, the regiment again went out on the same road, but not as far. They positioned themselves on the right side of the road and remained on picket duty in the woods during the night, returning to camp in the morning.

On November 3, 1864, new orders were received from New Orleans requiring the regiment to report to Saint Louis. Preparations were immediately made. The troops were very glad to get out of that cold and diseased environment. On the 4th, the 23rd, Wisconsin arrived at camp by boat and promptly relieved the Sixth Regiment.

On the 6th, the regiment embarked on the steamboat Thomas E. Tutt, for Saint Louis, arriving there on the 11th. It was said that it was a hard journey for the troops. Upon arriving they disembarked and marched through the city towards their temporary quarters (Winter Street Barracks), having real buildings to stay in. Duty in Saint Louis was miserable. The regiment was assigned to outside post and sentry duty guarding prisoners in the cold of winter. There was little protection from the cold.

On January 29, 1865, the regiment was ordered to report to New Orleans.

The next day they traveled by the Illinois Central Rail Road to Cairo, Illinois, Naval Base (Western Naval Headquarters). The trains unloaded the troops right next to the boats. From there, they boarded the steamboat W.R. Arthur. In all, the boat took on 1000 souls. She reached New Orleans on February 6, 1865.

When the boat arrived in Louisiana, the troops marched to their new quarters at Cotton Press No.1, which was used as a distribution camp. The Sixth Regiment was now attached to the Second Brigade of the Second Division, Sixteenth Army Corps, Major General A.J. Smith, Commanding. While in New Orleans the unit found that it was a strict military environment. Simply not having a pass when you leave camp would have meant imprisonment. New Orleans was a staging area for the union forces in the south. While in New Orleans the unit helped repair railroad tracks and buildings. They were relieved on March 3, 1865 by a colored troop detachment.

On March 6, 1865, the regiment left New Orleans and marched along the river to Chalmette, to a point a little below the old battlefield, located exactly opposite the Confederate breastworks. There they boarded a small ocean steamship called the Cromwell. The conditions aboard the ship were the worst. The troops were packed in so tight that one could not lay down. On March 8, 1865, the boat landed at Fort Gaines, Alabama. After disembarking they marched to a camping ground on the south shore of Dauphin Island, a small sandy barrier island, being about two miles west of the fort. Because they were in enemy territory, the cooks were pulled from duty and the troops were issued food rations to cook or do with as they pleased. On March 19, 1865, the regiment broke camp and embarked on a gunboat (Tin Clad). U.S.S. Meteor #44, under command of Master Meletiah Jordon. With noise and light restrictions in place, the boat lay all night in Navy Cove near Fort Morgan. The next day the fleet crossed to Fish River and traveled up it for several miles to a place called Dalney's Mill Landing.

The landing was located on the west side. After disembarking from the ship, the force traveled west for a short while and camped. The Second Brigade was about a mile away from the river on the south side, adjacent to a small but rapid creek. There breastworks were made facing towards the West.

UNITED STATES MILITARY RAILROAD
COURTESY WILLIAM C. DAVIS
THE BATTLEFIELDS OF THE CIVIL WAR

Throughout the night the regiment pickets could see the confederate pickets and likewise they saw us. Several shots were exchanged until morning. On that morning of the 27th, the rest of the regiment moved up and threw up breastworks. A battery was placed on the right flank. The regiment dug in for the night without further incident.

On the 28th, the regiment fell back to the south side of the creek where the Second Division was entrenched opposite the Sibley House. There was little to do during this entrenchment except to dig in even deeper and listen to the continuous cannonading at the Spanish Fort. The troops no longer made remarks about it because it seemed to be accepted, however plenty of comments were made when they could hear the rush of large shells coming from the rebel gun-boats.

On April 2, 1865, the Brigade conducted a reconnaissance (Recon) on the Blakely Road, to a point three miles out.

During the "recon", two torpedoes (land mines) were exploded at the feet of the horses at the head of the column. No other activity was found other than that event for this date.

On April 3, 1865, the Division broke camp and moved by way of Origen Sibley's Mills, to the front at Fort Blakely, on the Tensas River, which was about twelve miles from Mobile Alabama. They took position on the left flank of the Thirteenth Corps, which arrived there a couple of days earlier.

About one and a half miles to the East of the established rebel works that were set up to protect the town, was an unfenced graveyard setting among the pine trees. Immediately north of the graveyard resides a local family, the Wilkinson's. There home had a small piece of land about fifteen paces square, surrounded by a low brick wall. Here shortly after sunset on the 3rd of April, the Brigade encamped. The Sixth Minnesota were a couple of hundred paces south and southeast distant from the brick grave yard.

The troops were told not to pitch tents, light no fires, but lie on their arms, keeping as quiet as possible and await further orders. Rumor was that the rebel works would be stormed that night. The next day, 4th, tents were pitched and usual camp activities recommenced, except for the call of the bugle drum rolls.

While here and for the next week, a large detail of men were dispatched every day by the Regiment, for duty in the trenches and on the skirmish line. They would steel away before sunrise, each morning, the soldiers filed off through the gloomy ravines to their posts in the trenches, which was located about a half mile away. When they took up their positions they were to lie and exchange shots with the rebels and not budge even when hit by artillery shells.

On two or three occasions the men would climb the pine trees to catch a look at the enemy works and in retaliation the rebels would shell them.

The siege of Spanish Fort was well planned out. The force was led by General E.R.S. Canby. At the same time that the force was encircling Spanish Fort, the General knew that they only had 47 cannons and that for the most part they faced the bay. General Canby had 90 cannons and 32,000 men. He didn't know however, that the rebels only had 3,000 defenders. Simultaneously when this battle was being fought, a force of 13,000 union troops moved from Pensacola, Florida to break up the rail road connecting Mobile with Montgomery, this act completely encircled the confederate forces and opened the way for our troops to capture the Port of Mobile. This decisive battle would certainly help bring the war to an end.

ILLINOIS CENTRAL RAIL ROAD

WHARF BOATS THAT CARRIED
RASMUS'S REGIMENT

CAIRO, ILLINOIS NAVAL BASE CIRCA 1864
FOREGROUND IS A TRAIN AND AT SHORELINE ARE WHARF
BOATS THAT WERE PULLED BY THE STEAMBOATS THAT
CARRIED RASMUS'S REGIMENT

DOWNTOWN CAIRO (OHIO STREET) CIRCA 1864
COURTESY OF NATIONAL HISTORICAL SOCIETY

S.S. EMPRES
SCIRCA 1864
RASMUS TRAVELED FROM CAIRO, IL. TO HELENA AR.
ON THIS STEAMBOAT (NATIONAL ARCHIVES)

LANDING OF GENERAL CANBY'S 16TH CORP
FISH RIVER LANDING MARCH 1865
COURTESY FORT BLAKELY MUSEUM

Chapter Fourteen

APRIL 8, 1865-APRIL 9, 1865

BATTLE AT FORT BLAKELY

On April 8, 1865, starting at 5:30 p.m. until the hour of 7:00 p.m., a mass of shells were heard by Rasmus's regiment bombarding Fort Blakely. The average count was reported as thirty shells a minute. Much of the shelling came from gunboats in the bay, the gunboat that brought Rasmus to Fish River landing, was one of those boats. The force did little but dig in and wait for orders.

Around noon on April 9, the unit broke camp and the regiment left camp. At 4:00 p.m., the troops had their knapsacks on and moved with stealth through the woods towards the line of trenches used by the reserve picket guard where they took up their positions.

When the force arrived they piled all their knapsacks together, as was customary to lighten the soldiers burden during a fight. Having done that, they took up defensive fighting positions and awaited further orders. Immediately to the right of the Sixth defensive positioning was a cannon placement to protect their flank from attack. Beyond the cannon was another regiment. The enemy was about half mile west of the Sixth position and the forward troops were only 400 yards away. At 5:15 p.m., the Union opened up with all of their cannons, to include the cannon flanking the Sixth. About 25 minutes later the cannon fire halted and the forward trenched troops climbed out of their trenches yelling and whooping. Soon afterwards the Rebels surrendered under a white flag.

ATTACK ON FORT BLAKELY APRIL 9, 1865
COURTESY FORT BLAKELY MUSEUM

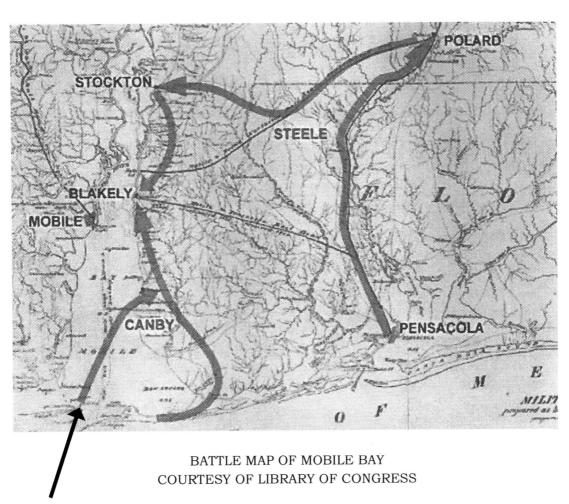

BATTLE MAP OF MOBILE BAY
COURTESY OF LIBRARY OF CONGRESS

RASMUS TOOK THIS ROUTE IN
THE GUNBOAT U.S. S. METEOR
TO FISH RIVER LANDING

"Author's Comments"

On April 9, 1865, just hours before the attack on Fort Blakely and Mobile, Confederate General Robert E. Lee, formally surrendered to Union General Ulysses S. Grant, in a small courthouse in Appomattox, Virginia. The War was over. The siege and capture of Fort Blakely was the last combined battle of the Civil War.

Had this been known at the time the Battle for Mobile was occurring, some 4700 lives would have been saved. In this author's opinion, the slavery of any man cannot be condoned, nor will it as long as we keep this great country strong. Also in my opinion, I believe that General Robert E. Lee was one of the greatest generals that ever lived. His tactical soldiering may never be matched. General Grant respected Lee to the point where he refused to take Lee's sword during the surrender ceremony.

RASMUS FOUGHT HERE

BREASTWORKS AT FORT BLAKELY
Author Photo

GRAVEYARD WHERE RASMUS CAMPED APRIL 3, 1865
Author Photo

Chapter Fifteen

MARCH 27,1865-APRIL 8, 1865

BATTLE AT SPANISH FORT

On March 25, 1865, Rasmus's Regiment broke camp and marched eight miles through enemy territory. The next day the 26th, the Second Brigade was positioned in the front of the column and Rasmus's Sixth Regiment was detailed to scout and skirmish the enemy in the woods. While engaged in this detail several small skirmishes erupted without casualties.

On the 27th, the Regiment was ordered to fall back. By noon they had crossed the creek that was at the old Sibley House and Mills and halted about a mile beyond that point of reference. The regiment was ordered to perform picket duty. They did so through-out the night and into the next day.

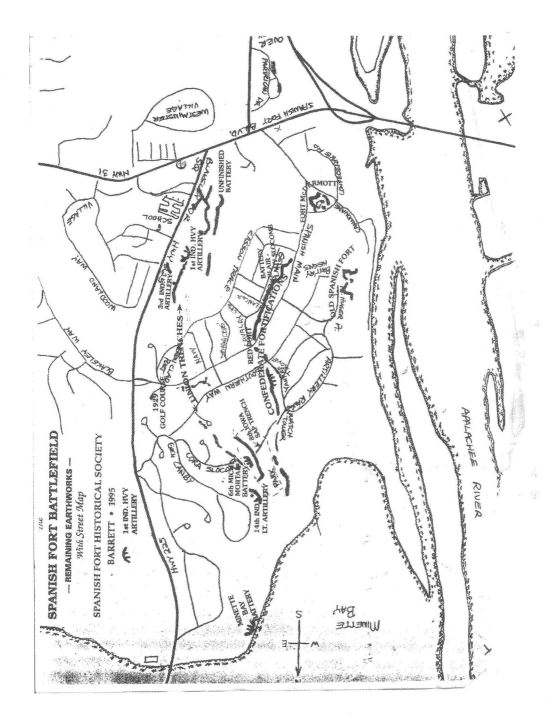

SPANISH FORT BATTLEFIELD

Chapter Sixteen

APRIL 12, 1865

OCCUPATION OF MOBILE

Following the Confederate surrender at Fort Blakely, the Sixth Minnesota moved forward and camped two days, deep behind what was once enemy lines. On April 12, the regiment arrived back at the old graveyard camp and remained there awaiting further orders. The next morning, the13th, and 16th Army Corp broke camp and began a northward march. The route covered some Sixty miles, through pine forests having little or no clearings. They passed the towns of Burnt Corn, Midway, Activity, Greenville and Sandy Ridge. As they passed by the houses in these towns, they observed that most of the houses posted a white cloth or flag, many bearing the words "The Union Forever".

On April 19, 1865, just before midnight, news finally reached the camp that General Lee had surrendered. On April 24, 1865, they heard rumors that President Abraham Lincoln was shot and killed. Not everyone believed the rumor. The regiment continued their march north for the next 13 days, arriving on the 25th of April, at a stream, located five miles south of Montgomery. They had traveled some 170 miles since camping at the graveyard at Fort Blakely. On the 26th of April, the troops camped and washed there clothing.

On the 27th of April, the Brigade marched through the City of Montgomery and set up camp a few miles out of town, just below a swamp on River Road.

They remained there until May 18, at which time they broke camp and moved it one mile further up river to Wetumka Road, doing this for higher ground and purer water.

The regiment remained in Montgomery as an occupying force until July 1865. Everyone was more than anxious to get home.

On July 16, 1865, they broke camp, having been ordered to Vicksburg to muster out of service. They boarded the Steamship Coquette, heading for Selma, Alabama. The next morning the Brigade arrived in Selma. On July 20, 1865, the Brigade departed from Selma by railroad towards Demopolis, arriving there in the afternoon. Because the railroads and bridges had been blown up during the war, travel required a lot of walking from where the damage occurred until it was usable again. They had to embark on a steamship that brought them four miles, where they again boarded the railroad, on the west bank. The Brigade traveled to McDowell's Landing where they camped for the night.

The next day they traveled to Meridian, Mississippi, where they stayed the night. The next day, July 22nd, they again traveled, this time to Pearl River, near Jackson.

On July 25, 1865, nearly all of the regiment had rendezvous on the west side of the Big Black River. The next day they boarded railroad cars.

They headed for Vicksburg. From there they embarked on the Steamboat Missouri, arriving in Saint Louis on July 31, 1865, where upon arrival they received orders to report to Fort Snelling.

On August 1, 1865, they embarked on the Steamship Brillant, for Saint Paul, Minnesota. They arrived on August 7th and were promptly met by greeting citizens. The regiment was entertained by the governor. On August 19, 1865, the unit mustered out of federal service at Fort Snelling.

This concluded the military service for Rasmus Olson. He served honorably under the most horrible conditions possible. This country owes him a debt of gratitude as it does to all of his regiment, and all of the military services of this great country of ours, past, present and future. For without them we would not be free.

The Sixth Minnesota Volunteer Infantry lost 12 enlisted men, killed and mortally wounded and 4 officers and 161 men died of disease. Total 177

FISH RIVER LANDING PIER PILINGS IN FOREGROUND
FACING TOWARDS DAUPHIN ISLAND CIRCA 2009

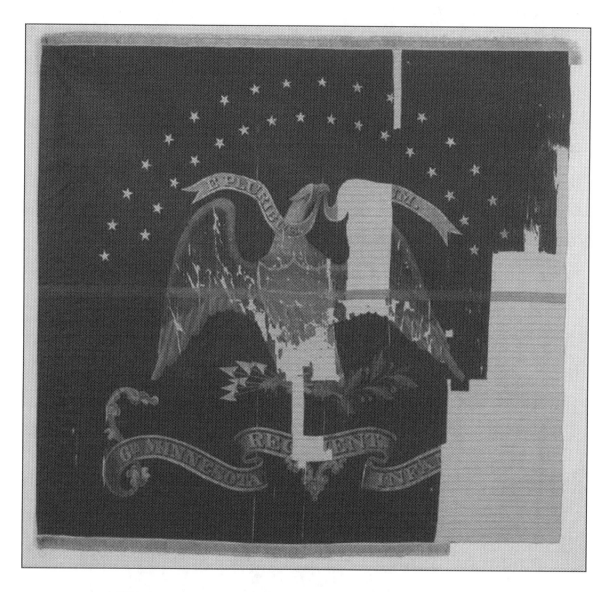

ACTUAL BATTLE FLAG OF THE SIXTH MINNESOTA INFANTRY
COURTESY OF MINNESOTA HISTORICAL SOCIETY

Chapter Seventeen

1665-1893

GENEALOGY OF RASMUS

LOUIS OLSON
BROTHER OF RASMUS
CIRCA 1870 Family Album

Sometime between August 19, 1865 and June 1, 1880, Rasmus and
Caroline accumulated approximately 160 acres of land in Minnesota and

farmed on it. On June 1, 1880, according to the 1880 United States Census, Rasmus and Caroline resided at 270 Halsted Street, Chicago, Cook County, Illinois. They lived with John and Olive Nelson (Rasmus's daughter) and Emma Nelson (Olives daughter). John lists his occupation as a lather, Elizabeth and Caroline as keeping house and Rasmus as a laborer. At this point in time Rasmus was 55 years old.

Carolyn reported on the 1900 U.S. Census, that she gave birth to six children and that as of 1900, only Olive was living. The author has not been able to ascertain who the other five children were because the Great Chicago Fire destroyed the records. His child (Olive) gave birth to Emma Nelson and to Mabel Rena Nelson, who had five daughters;

RASMUS OLSON
February 19, 1825-November 22, 1893
Circa 1870 Family Album

CAROLINE LARSON
BORN DECEMBER 2, 1839 DIED OCTOBER 25,1905
MARRIED RASMUS OLSON MARCH 29, 1857 Family Album

OLIVE ELIZABETH OLSON
DAUGHTER OF RASMUS OLSON
BORN APRIL 1859 DIED AUGUST 23, 1939
MARRIED JOHN NELSON OCTOBER 23, 1875
CIRCA 1898 Family Album

JOHN NELSON
BORN MAY 1854 DIED MAY 2, 1905
OLIVES HUSBAND CIRCA 1898
Family Album

MABLE RENA NELSON
DAUGHTER OF OLIVE E. NELSON (OLSON)
BORN JANUARY 17, 1885 DIED MAY 19, 1979
MARRIED HARRY CHRISTENSEN NOVEMBER 25, 1912
CIRCA 1903 Family Album

HARRY CHRISTENSEN
MABEL'S HUSBAND
BORN APRIL 26, 1885 DIED OCTOBER 17, 1955
CIRCA 1910 Family Album

HELEN MARJORIE CHRISTENSEN
BORN AUGUST 13, 1921 DIED JANUARY 28, 2008
MARRIED JAMES JOSEPH BORN JULY 1, 1944
CIRCA 1976 Family Album

JAMES JOSEPH BORN JR.
HELEN'S HUSBAND
BORN JULY 26, 1923 DIED MAY 17, 2009
CIRCA 1944 Family Album

JAMES THOMAS BORN
SON OF JIM AND HELEN BORN
HUSBAND OF BECKY
AUTHOR CIRCA 1964 Family Album

BECKY SUE BORN (SOUTHARD)
AUTHOR'S WIFE
BORN JANUARY 31, 1949
CIRCA 1966 Family Album

HEATHER LINNEA BORN
BORN APRIL 20, 1976
DAUGHTER OF JIM AND BECKY BORN
GREAT-GREAT-GREAT GRANDDAUGHTER OF RASMUS
CIRCA 1994 Family Album

MARK DANIEL BORN
BORN JULY 15, 1977
SON OF JIM AND BECKY BORN
GREAT-GREAT-GREAT GRANDSON OF RASMUS
CIRCA 2011 Family Album

**Pedigree Chart for
Rasmus Olson**

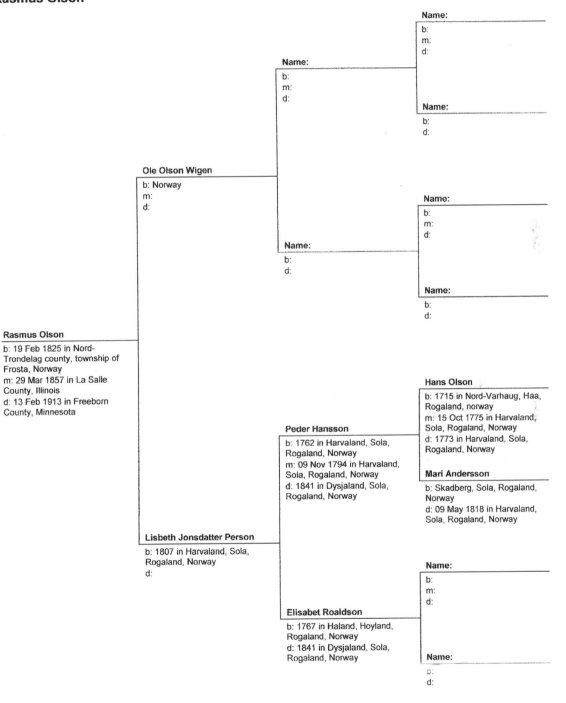

Rasmus Olson

b: 19 Feb 1825 in Nord-Trondelag county, township of Frosta, Norway
m: 29 Mar 1857 in La Salle County, Illinois
d: 13 Feb 1913 in Freeborn County, Minnesota

Ole Olson Wigen

b: Norway
m:
d:

Name:
b:
m:
d:

Name:
b:
m:
d:

Name:
b:
d:

Name:
b:
m:
d:

Name:
b:
d:

Name:
b:
d:

Lisbeth Jonsdatter Person

b: 1807 in Harvaland, Sola, Rogaland, Norway
d:

Peder Hansson

b: 1762 in Harvaland, Sola, Rogaland, Norway
m: 09 Nov 1794 in Harvaland, Sola, Rogaland, Norway
d: 1841 in Dysjaland, Sola, Rogaland, Norway

Hans Olson

b: 1715 in Nord-Varhaug, Haa, Rogaland, norway
m: 15 Oct 1775 in Harvaland, Sola, Rogaland, Norway
d: 1773 in Harvaland, Sola, Rogaland, Norway

Mari Andersson

b: Skadberg, Sola, Rogaland, Norway
d: 09 May 1818 in Harvaland, Sola, Rogaland, Norway

Elisabet Roaldson

b: 1767 in Haland, Hoyland, Rogaland, Norway
d: 1841 in Dysjaland, Sola, Rogaland, Norway

Name:
b:
m:
d:

Name:
b:
d:

James T Born

Hans Olson

b: 1715 in Nord-Varhaug, Haa, Rogaland,
norway
m: 15 Oct 1775 in Harvaland, Sola,
Rogaland, Norway
d: 1773 in Harvaland, Sola, Rogaland,
Norway

1

Ola Hansson

b: Abt. 1679 in Skjaerpe, Haa, Rogaland,
Norway
m: Nord-Varhaug, Haa, Rogaland, norway
d: 1740 in Nord-Varhaug, Haa, Rogaland,
norway

Elisabet Rasmusson

b: Abt. 1680 in Norway
d:

Hans Olson

b: 1640 in Skjærpe, Hå, Rogaland, Norway
m: Skjaerpe, Haa, Rogaland, Norway
d: Skjaerpe, Haa, Rogaland, Norway

Sissel Ivarson

b: Abt. 1657 in Risa, Haa, Rogaland,
Norway
d:

Rasmus Olson

b: 1640 in RE, Time, Rogaland, Norway
m:
d: 1701 in Nord Varhaug, Haa, Rogaland,
Norway

Eli Pedersdtr

b: Nord Varhaug, Hå, Rogaland, Norway
d:

Name:
b:
m:
d:

Name:
b:
d:

Anders Olsson
b: 07 May 1734 in Tjora, Sola, Rogaland, Norway
m:
d: 1734 in Skadberg, Sola, Rogaland, Norway

Mari Andersson
b: Skadberg, Sola, Rogaland, Norway
m: 15 Oct 1775 in Harvaland, Sola, Rogaland, Norway
d: 09 May 1818 in Harvaland, Sola, Rogaland, Norway

1

Anna Johannesson
b: Erga, Klepp, Rogaland, Norway
d: 1774 in Skadberg, Sola, Rogaland, Norway

Johannes Eivindson
b: 1665 in Erga, Klepp, Rogaland, Norway
m:
d: 1749 in Erga, Klepp, Rogaland, Norway

Eli Eivindson
b: Hauge, Klepp, Rogaland, Norway
d: Erga, Klepp, Rogaland, Norway

CHILDREN OF HARRY CHRISTENSEN AND
MABEL RENEA NELSON

GREAT-GRANDDAUGHTERS *OF RASMUS OLSON*

OLIVE MARIE CHRISTENSEN 9-26-1913 6-12-1973

DOROTHY MABEL CHRISTENSEN 8-13-1921 11-14-2001

BERNICE LILLIAN CHRISTENSEN 10-31-1915 9-29-2002

JUNE HARRIET CHRISTENSEN 6-28-1924 3-5-2001

HELEN MARJORIE CHRISTENSEN 8-13-1921 1-28-2008

GREAT-GREAT GRANDCHILDREN
OF
RASMUS OLSON

MOTHER: CHILD:

OLIVE   **NO CHILDREN**

BERNICE   **SANDRA LEE HAGEN**
                           1942-LIVING
                           RONALD HARRY HAGEN
                           1939-1989

DOROTHY   **JANIE HELEN KUTANSKY**
                           1945-LIVING
                           JOANNE OLIVE KUTANSKY
                           1949-LIVING

HELEN   **JAMES THOMAS BORN**
                           1946-LVING
                           MICHAEL JOHN BORN
                           1948-LIVING
                           CANDICE HOPE BORN
                           1950-1977
                           HOLLY FAITH BORN
                           1964-LIVING

JUNE   **KAREN MARIE JOHNSON**
                           1948-LIVING
                           NANCY ANN JOHNSON
                           1952-LIVING

NOTE:

Dorothy and Helen were twins, Dorothy was first born. Helen was believed to be born dead, at which time her doctor placed her into a suit case, which was then placed under my grandmothers bed. Soon after, my grandmother kept insisting that her daughter was alive, and to calm her, they opened the suit case only to find Helen alive and well. Helen went on to outlive them all.

Chapter Eighteen

ANSWERING A CALL TO ARMS

Rasmus Olson, like those who came before and after him, stepped forward when our country asked for men to take up arms to defend her freedom. This chapter is dedicated to my family members who left their jobs, left behind their mother's, father's, wives and children and were willing to sacrifice their own lives, so that you and me can live free in this great country of ours. When you look at the American Flag next time, keep in mind and in reverence that the flags red stripes, represent the blood that was shed by so many, so that you can be free to live where you want, to do what you want, and to be a free person. I don't know who it was that said "Freedom isn't free", but they certainly knew what they were talking about.

While I have a great many more relatives that answered the call to arms, I am lacking their photographs to show you. Some but not all of them excluded in this chapter, are Bertram A. Gelb (U.S. Army), and his twin brother Leonard P. Gelb (U.S. Army) both served in the famed Rainbow Division in WWII Europe, both received the Bronze Star Medal. John Nelson's (Spanish American War) son Carl John Nelson served in World War II (see photo) and ultimately died of his wounds. He received the Bronze Star Medal and two Purple Hearts for action while liberating the City of Rome, Italy. Carl's son John Carl Nelson, (U.S. Army) served in Cam Ranh Bay, Vietnam with my brother Michael.

My father James J. Born Jr., was at Pearl Harbor, fought in the Battle of Midway, Guam, Wake Island Iwo Jima and Okinawa. He was wounded by a Japanese Betty Bomber that was trying to blow up a barge he was on in New Guinea. The list goes on and I salute their service and courage. May your off spring step forward to answer the call to arms.

WALL OF HONOR
FAMILY RELATIONS, WHO LIKE RASMUS,
ANSWERED THE CALL TO ARMS

RASMUS OLSON U.S. ARMY 1862-1865
AMERICAN INDIAN WARS AND U.S. CIVIL WAR
Family Album

WALL OF HONOR
FAMILY RELATIONS, WHO LIKE RASMUS,
ANSWERED THE CALL TO ARMS

JOHN NELSON U.S. ARMY 1898-1890
CUBA INVASION
SPANISH AMERICAN WAR
Family Album

WALL OF HONOR
FAMILY RELATIONS, WHO LIKE RASMUS,
ANSWERED THE CALL TO ARMS

JAMES J. BORN Jr. U.S. NAVY 1940-1960
SOUTH PACIFIC THEATRE SUBMARINES
U.S.S. Sailfish
WORLD WAR II AND KOREAN WAR

119

WALL OF HONOR

JOSEPH S. KUTANSKY U.S. ARMY
EUROPEAN THEATRE—BATTLE OF THE BULGE
WORLD WAR II

<u>WALL OF HONOR</u>
FAMILY MEMBERS, WHO LIKE RASMUS,
ANSWERED THE CALL TO ARMS

ARNOLD J. FLOBECK (center) U.S. NAVY
PACIFIC THEATRE MINE MAN
<u>WORLD WAR II</u>

WALL OF HONOR
FAMILY MEMBERS, WHO LIKE RASMUS,
ANSWERED THE CALL TO ARMS

ROBERT G. JOHNSON U.S. ARMY AIR CORPS
EUROPEAN THEATRE-TAIL GUNNER
WORLD WAR II

<u>WALL OF HONOR</u>
FAMILY MEMBERS, WHO LIKE RASMUS,
ANSWERED THE CALL TO ARMS

CLIFFORD J. NELSON U.S. ARMY
EUROPEAN THEATRE-LIBERATED ROME, ITALY
LATER DIED OF WOUNDS RECEIVED
85th Infantry (Custer Division)
<u>WORLD WAR II</u>

WALL OF HONOR
FAMILY MEMBERS, WHO LIKE RASMUS,
ANSWERED THE CALL TO ARMS

ROBERT P. NESS U.S. ARMY AIR CORPS
EUROPEAN THEATRE—BOMBED GERMANY
WORLD WAR II
B29 BOMBER PILOT

JAMES T. BORN U.S. NAVY
SEAL TEAM II ASSAULT BOAT CAPTAIN
MEKONG DELTA, <u>VIETNAM WAR</u>

MICHAEL J. BORN U.S. NAVY
COMBAT PHOTOGRAPHER—CAM RANH BAY
<u>VIETNAM WAR</u>

SEAN M. GILLESPIE U.S. ARMY
SON OF MICHAEL J. BORN
MUNITIONS EXPERT
<u>CIRCA WAR ON IRAQ ERA</u>

RASMUS OLSON PARTIAL FAMILY DESCENDANTS
GREAT GRANDCHILDREN DOWN TO GGG GRANDCHILDREN
CIRCA 1982
MAIDEN NAMES

GRAND CHILD
GREAT-GREAT GRAND CHILD
3RD GREAT GRANDCHILD
4TH GREAT GRAND CHILD

1 Jeffrey St. Ours	14 **Holly Born**	27 Sharon Hagen
2 **Karen Johnson**	15 **Sandy Hagen**	
3 **Joann Kutansky**	16 James J. Born	
4 Matthew Crum	17 **Helen Christensen**	
5 James St. Ours	18 **Bernice Christensen**	
6 **June Christensen**	19 Thomas Mc Gough	
7 Robert Johnson	20 Ronald Hagen	
8 **Janie Kutansky**	21 Megan Crum	
9 Arnold Flobeck	22 Matthew Crum	
10 Robyn Hagen	23 Jason Graf	
11 Lindale Graf	24 Jennifer Graf	
12 Robert Killam	25 **Dorothy Christensen**	
13 Joseph Kutansky	26 Courtney Kozik	

Sometime after Carolyn's death in Chicago, Rasmus moved back to Minnesota and later to California. He was a member of Lyon Post No.8, in Oakland, California. According to an 1886 Grand Army of the Republic, Post No. 8. Directory, he lived at 908 Willow Street, in Oakland, California, where today stands a large rectangular, abandoned, grass and dirt lot, surrounded by a chain length fence.

Rasmus worked as a carpenter by trade. He attended meetings every Tuesday, at the Grand Army Hall, at 419 13th St. Rasmus remained active in his community. On August 11, 1892, he registered to vote, as evidence of the official Voter Registry for Alameda County, First Ward, Precinct No.3.

According to this source, Rasmus was five foot ten inches in height, having a florid complexion (medically defined as a ruddy healthy reddish color, often associated with outdoor life, as in the appearance of the rosy cheeks of Santa Claus), having blue eyes and gray hair. He was reported as naturalized as a citizen of the United States on November 1850, in Waukesha County, Illinois.

On November 22, 1893, at the age of 67, Rasmus passed away in his home, at 1713 Goss Street, Oakland, California. The cause of death, as found on his death certificate, was Hepatic Cirrhosis. In re-searching this disease in a medical dictionary, I learned that it was a chronic degenerative disease of the liver, in which normal cells are damaged and then replaced by scar tissue. The most common cause for this disease is excessive consumption of alcoholic beverages. This may give us a clue as to his life style, at least in the latter part of his years.

Taking into account his past military combat experience, the horrors he lived through, his continued attendance at the GAR meetings for like companionship of fellow soldiers, and his apparent heavy drinking problem, he may very well have suffered from Post Traumatic Stress Disorder (PTSD), common to soldiers of all wars. During his period of military service, PTSD was called "Shell Shock". This term was changed to PTSD sometime towards the end of the Vietnam War.

Rasmus is now at peace. He is buried in the Grand Army of the Republic Plot, in the Mountain view Cemetery, Oakland, California, with his fellow soldiers, many of whom suffered the same fate.

Of mentioning, in 1871, Rasmus and Caroline lived in Chicago with their daughter Olive. As best as I can determine from old directories and fragments of records, their house was located about two blocks above Mrs. O'Leary's house, where the famed cow was reported to have kicked over a lantern in the shed, sparking the Great Chicago Fire.

Story's have been passed down that the family sat in a wagon in the Chicago River down by the stock yards, and watched the city burn. Olive was only twelve years old then. She supposedly composed a good bye letter as the fire neared. As of this writing no evidence of that fact has been found. Unfortunately the city census and records establishing proof of residence were all destroyed in the fire. Perhaps in time, more proof of this story will come to light.

According to the National Archives Records Administration, for Deceased Union Civil War Veterans, his grave site headstone was ordered on November 30, 1894 (a year after his death) and was manufactured by the Vermont Marble Company, in Proctor, Vermont

The Great Chicago Fire, Courtesy of Harpers Weekly

For historical perspective, the Chicago fire started around nine at night, on October 8, 1871 (Sunday), at or around 137 Dekoven Street, Chicago. It burned until Tuesday, October 10, 1871. Hundreds were forced to flee to the river and lake. The waterfronts, especially Lake Michigan were crowded. Most everyone was in a panic.

Any area where there was water, was crowded with people and horse-drawn wagons, being filled with furniture, people and their personal belongings. To keep from burning they drove their wagons into the river. It has been told that Rasmus and his family were one of those families that sat it out in the river down by the stock yards.

TRIBUTE TO THE MAN

All of us have hero's that we admire, and from time to time we look up to them to set an example for what we are supposed to do in our life. We are forever seeking the correct paths in life and for most of us, strive to better ourselves. Men like Rasmus are the type of hero that we should gravitate to mimic. For it is great men like Rasmus, that helped to give birth to this great Nation of ours, and gave us the freedoms that many of us take for granted, and all of us enjoy today.

James T. Born

Conclusion
RASMUS OLSON STORY

According to the United States General Land Office, on August 5, 1869, by Act of Congress, page 329, Certificate No. 7072, Rasmus acquired 40 acres of land, in Winnebago, Minnesota. The land was given to him and the certificate bears the name of President Ulysses S. Grant.

On October 25, 1905, Rasmus's wife Caroline, at the age of 66, passed away quietly at her home, having out lived her husband by twelve years.

My grandmother, Mabel Renea Nelson (January 17, 1885-May 19, 1979), Born in Chicago and Died in Los Angeles, CA) and her brother Carl John Nelson, born in Illinois (December 2, 1889) and died in Hennepin County, Minnesota (May 27, 1966), who livedjust a county away from where Rasmus used to live and just two counties away from where he had his first Indian engagement.

GRAND ARMY OF THE REPUBLIC PLOT
MONUMENT (Oakland, California)
Photo Courtesy of Kari Petersen

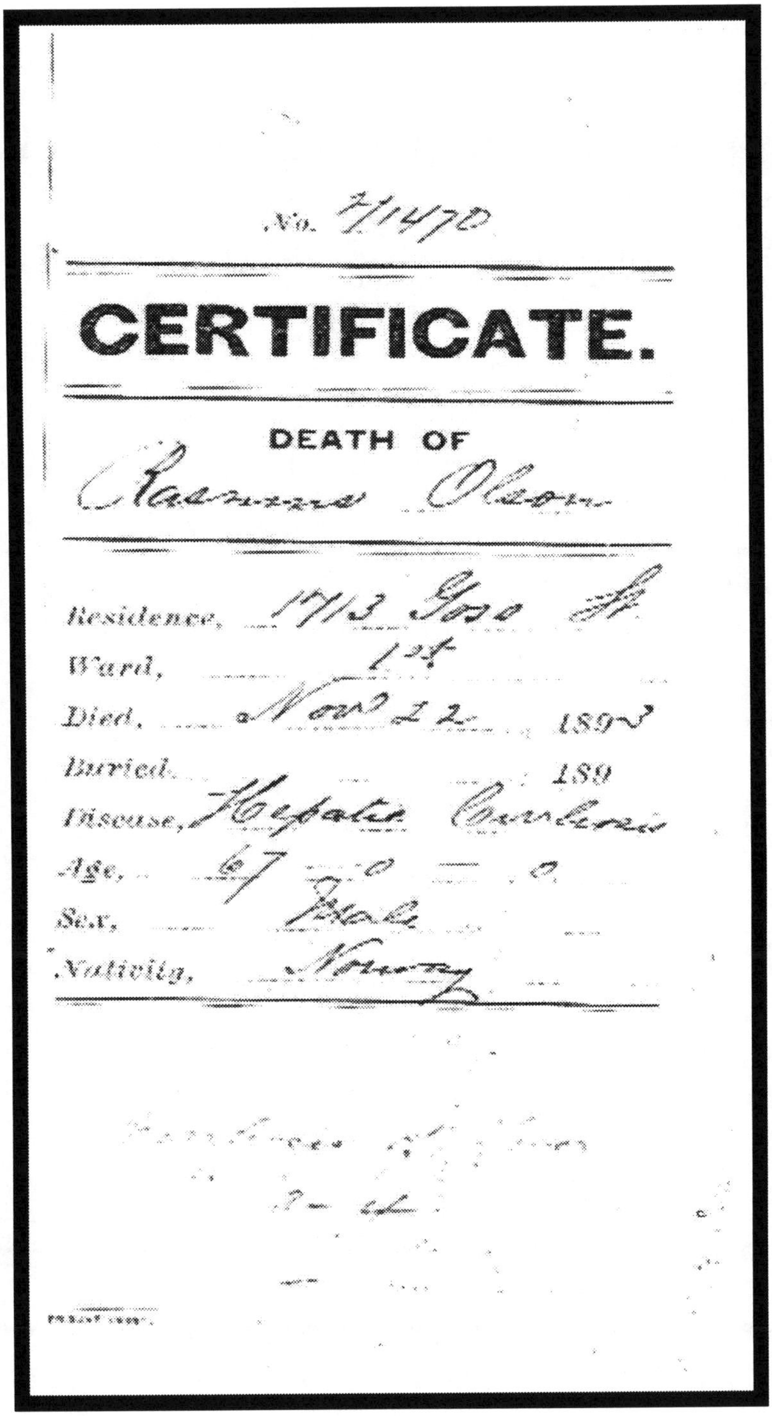

No. 71470

CERTIFICATE.

DEATH OF

Rasmus Olson

Residence, 1713 Goso St.

Ward, 1st

Died, Nov 22 1893

Buried, 189

Disease, Hepatic Carlinex

Age, 67 0 0

Sex, Male

Nativity, Norway

PHOTO COURTESY OF KARI PETERSEN

135

RASMUS DEATH CERTIFICATE
PHOTO COURTESY OF KARI PETERSEN

GRAVE STONE MARKER
OF RASMUS OLSON
Photo Courtesy of Kari Petersen
Circa 2011

It is the soldier,
not the President,
who gives us Democracy,

It is the soldier,
not the Congress,
who takes care of us.

It is the soldier,
not the reporter,
who has given us Freedom of Press.

It is the soldier,
not the poet,
who has given us Freedom of Speech,

It is the soldier,
not the campus organizer,
who has given us the freedom to demonstrate.

It is the soldier,
who salutes the flag,
who serves beneath the flag,
and whose coffin is draped by the flag,
that allows the protester to burn the flag.

Father Dennis O'Brien
United States Marine Corp., Chaplin

INDIAN WAR CAMPAIGN MEDAL
Awarded to Rasmus Olson for his participation in the
Indian Wars of 1862-1864.

CIVIL WAR CAMPAIGN MEDAL
Awarded to Rasmus Olson for his service in the
United States Army, during the period 1862-1865

FORT RIDGELY CAMPAIGN MEDAL
Awarded to Rasmus Olson, for defending Fort Ridgely,
during the Sioux Indian attack August 18-27, 1862

PURPLE HEART MEDAL
Awarded to Rasmus Olson, for wounds received in
battle, while at Birch Coulee, August 20-22, 1862

RASMUS OLSON
PATRIOT